KU-472-733

Antiques

GUINNESS BOOKS

EDITOR: Beatrice Frei
DESIGN AND LAYOUT: Alan Hamp

Published in Great Britain by Guinness Publishing Ltd,
33 London Road, Enfield, Middlesex

Typeset in England by
Dorchester Typesetting Group Ltd

Printed and bound in Portugal by Printer Portuguesa

British Library Cataloguing in Publication Data

Feild, Rachel
Guinness antiques: pocket price guide
1. Antiques
I. Title
745.1 NK1125

ISBN 0-85112-380-5

Contents

ACKNOWLEDGEMENTS

The publisher would like to thank Phillips Fine Art Auctioneers for the use of all the photographs in this book with the exception of those on p. 39 which were supplied by Alan Hamp.
The prices given are not those for any item fetched at auction but represent only a guide to the prices of similar objects in a good, reliable antique shop dealing in good quality, middle range objects.

RACHAEL FEILD has spent most of her working life in magazines and journalism. She began writing about antiques about ten years ago, and her first book, written in collaboration with Rupert Gentle, was the definitive *English Domestic Brass 1680–1810*. She has contributed to many of the major antiques magazines including a series of articles for *Connoisseur*. Rachael Feild is the author of the *Which? Guide to Buying Antiques* published by The Consumers' Association, *Irons in the Fire* – a History of Cooking Equipment published by Crowood Press and, most recently, *Buying Antique Furniture* published by Macdonald which featured in the *Sunday Times* bestseller list. For the last three years she has also contributed a regular monthly feature on prices and trends in the London and provincial salerooms for *Antique Dealer & Collectors' Guide* as well as many other articles on specialist subjects.

Phillips
Fine Art Auctioneers

Phillips Fine Art Auctioneers have the largest and most comprehensive network of salerooms throughout the British Isles, with twenty saleroom branches offering a full range of services, from Scotland to Cornwall, Wales to East Anglia. Each regional office is self-contained and is run on individual lines, with regular sales calendars for antiques and objets d'art from the surrounding area. It is not Phillips' policy to cream off the best objects to send down to their London salerooms, except on rare occasions when, in their capacity as agents for the vendors, they consider that a better price would be obtained. This is by no means the rule, since many regions have built up their own specialist sales which are regularly attended by important collectors and private buyers from all over the country. Thus every region has the full benefit of Phillips' expertise and can be assured of the highest standards of service to both buyer and seller. In addition, Phillips hold regular road shows when teams of experts visit towns and cities to advise and value an incredibly wide range of antiques and objets d'art brought to them by members of the public.

Phillips were established in 1796: many of their regional salerooms are continuations of even older firms of fine art auctioneers which have now become members of the Phillips group, using the same strict conditions of sale and maintaining the same high standards of practice. In recent years, Phillips has built up many of the smaller specialist categories into sales of considerable importance. Of these, Doulton pottery, Art Nouveau and Art Deco ceramics and glass, Studio ceramics, British watercolours, and decorative prints have been among the most successful, while Phillips' sales of dolls, toys, model soldiers and early clockwork toys are now established as among the most important to be held regularly in the U.K.

The wide and varied range of more regular items can be seen in the pages of this Pocket Guide. All illustrations have been carefully chosen from Phillips' extensive photographic library of objects which have passed through their salerooms in the last two years – a small representation of the £60.5 million turnover achieved in 1985. Phillips also have a comprehensive coverage of the international field and have salerooms in New York and offices in Boston, Brussels, Geneva, Paris and Toronto.

SALEROOMS

Phillips – London
Blenstock House,
7 Blenheim Street,
New Bond Street,
London W1Y 0AS
Tel: 01-629 6602
Telex: 298855 Blen G

Marylebone
Hayes Place,
Lisson Grove,
London NW1 6UA
Tel: 01-723 2647

West 2
10 Salem Road,
Bayswater W2 4BU
Tel: 01-221 5303

Phillips – Bath
1 Old King Street,
Bath BA1 2JT
Tel: 0225 310609/310709

Phillips – Cardiff
9–10 Westgate Street,
Cardiff CF1 1DA
Tel: 0222 396453

Phillips – Chester
New House,
150 Cristleton Road,
Chester,
Cheshire CH3 5TD
Tel: 0244 313936/7

Phillips – Colwyn Bay
9 Conwy Road,
Colwyn Bay, Clwyd LL29 7AF
Tel: 0492 533406

Phillips – Cornwall
Eastcliffe Road,
Cornubia Hall,
Par, Cornwall PL24 2AQ
Tel: 0726 81 4047/8/9

Phillips – Exeter
Alphin Brook Road,
Exeter, Devon EX2 8HT
Tel: 0392 39025/6

Phillips – Folkestone
11 Bayle Parade,
Folkestone, Kent CT20 1SQ
Tel: 0303 45555

Phillips – Ipswich
Dover House,
Wolsey Street,
Ipswich IP1 1UD
Tel: 0473 55137

50 St. Nicholas Street,
Ipswich IP1 1TP
Tel: 0473 54664

Phillips – Knowle
The Old House,
Station Road,
Knowle, Solihull,
West Midlands B93 0HT
Tel: 056 45 6151

Phillips – Leeds
17a East Parade,
Leeds, West Yorkshire
LS1 2BU
Tel: 0532 448011

Phillips – Morley
20 Fountain Street,
Morley, Leeds
LS27 9EN
Tel: 0532 523888

Phillips – Oxford
39 Park End Street,
Oxford OX1 1JD
Tel: 0865 723524

Phillips – Plymouth
Armada Street,
North Hill,
Plymouth PL4 8LS
Tel: 0752 673504

Phillips – Scotland
65 George Street,
Edinburgh EH2 2JL
Tel: 031 225 2266

207 Bath Street,
Glasgow G2 4HD
Tel: 041 221 8377

Phillips – Sherborne
Long Street Salerooms,
Sherborne, Dorset DT9 3BS
Tel: 0935 815271

OFFICES

Phillips – Barnstaple
10 Taw Vale,
Barnstaple, North Devon
EX32 8NJ
Tel: 0271 74481

Phillips – Cambridge
The Golden Rose,
17 Emmanuel Road,
Cambridge CB1 1JW
Tel: 0223 66523

Phillips – Carlisle
48 Cecil Street,
Carlisle, Cumbria CA1 1NT
Tel: 0228 42422

Phillips – Carmarthen
33 Kings Street,
Carmarthen, Dyfed
Tel: 0267 238231

Phillips – Melbourne
1 Chapel Street,
Melbourne,
Derbyshire DE7 1EU
Tel: 03316 3761

Phillips – Norwich
3 Opie Street, Norwich
Norfolk NR1 3DP
Tel: 0603 616426

Phillips – Rochdale
19 Drake Street,
Rochdale OL16 1RE
Tel: 0706 251004

OVERSEAS

Phillips – New York
406 East 79th Street,
New York NY 10021 USA
Tel: 212 570 4830
Telex: 126380 Bids NYK

Phillips – Geneva
Phillips, Son & Neale SA
6 rue de la Cité
1204 Geneva, Switzerland
Tel: 41 22 28-68-28
Telex: 229 85 Vif CH

Phillips – Paris
38 rue de Penthièvre
(Faubourg Saint-Honoré)
75008 Paris
Tel: 33 1 45 62 76 66

Phillips – Brussels
15 Avenue de Putdael,
1105 Brussels
Tel: 32 2 771 9852

Phillips – Netherlands
Lange Vijverberg 4/5,
2513 AC The Hague
Tel: 70 639900

Phillips – Zurich
Nicolas Beurret,
Rämistrasse 27,
8001 Zurich
Tel: 12 52 69 62

Introduction

Most people who embark on buying antiques know a little about the subject and, in general terms, what it is they want to buy: a piece of silver, a set of chairs, a clock, a desk or a piece of porcelain. They seldom set out at the beginning to become experts, collectors or buyers of more than one or two things. Maybe they have become householders for the first time, or they need to refurnish a room, or have a little money to spend on something which will give pleasure as well as appreciate in value over the years. In theory it seems a simple matter. But all too often they find the choice alarmingly large, alarmingly different in price and exceedingly hard to understand.

Legislation and consumer protection in recent years has in a way made life more difficult for the prospective buyer rather than more simple. Antiques are not an exact science, and descriptions in catalogues and on labels and tickets are necessarily vague because the law requires provable facts and in the world of antiques these are often few and far between. It is up to the buyer to ask the questions, which will be answered most willingly and helpfully and indeed are essential if misunderstandings are not to occur.

Obviously it is not possible within the compass of such a small book to include every piece of information, every price and every article. Shelves of books in libraries and great tomes of prices of objects which have passed through the salerooms testify to that fact. It is possible, however, to distil the basic facts about the whole complex field into an easily readable, understandable form, so that anyone venturing out into the world of antiques is equipped with a general idea of price, period, form and value. Armed with this knowledge they will neither feel ignorant nor foolish and, by knowing the right questions to ask, will be able to avoid the major mistakes and pitfalls of the market.

Where to start

This guide is not, in the sense that most guides are, solely a price guide, nor is it crammed with useful but unconnected pieces of information which may further confuse the buyer. The aim of this guide is to help the potential antique-buyer firstly to identify in general terms the different periods, styles and designs of furniture, silver, clocks, pottery, porcelain and glass. And secondly to give guidelines which can safely be followed concerning the current prices a buyer can expect to pay in a good, reliable antique shop dealing in good quality middle-range objects.

Each section is set out in chronological order, so that changing styles can be seen in their proper progression. Names of the best-known makers, together with their dates, can be referred to quickly and easily. Different woods used in cabinet-making are listed, with the periods during which each was most commonly used. The various stages in the development of pottery through to 'porcelain' are shown with typical examples, together with an explanation of the precise difference between all the various 'bodies' from pottery to stoneware to soft-paste and hard-paste porcelain to bone china. The development of movements in clocks, both longcase, lantern and bracket is traced, with examples of all the various stages. The use and meaning of hallmarks on silver is explained, and the growth of the glass industry in England from the first use of 'lead glass' or 'flint glass' instead of Continental soda glass which it almost totally replaced. And there is a simple guide to the prices you may expect to pay, depending on condition, fluctuations in the market, and availability.

Catalogues of saleroom prices, either in London or in the provinces, are useful reference books, particularly for the trade, but to a beginner they may often be misleading. Saleroom prices everywhere are as difficult to predict as the English weather – and can produce equally baffling results. Quite often the prices realized depend as much on who attends the sale as on what is being sold. To give an example: on one day, a piece of porcelain may be the object of intense competition between two dealers or collectors, both prepared to pay almost anything to acquire it. Some time later at another saleroom, an almost identical object can sell for less than half the price, because the competition is not there. Somewhere in between those two extremes lies the price a good antique dealer will be asking.

To a certain extent that price will be affected by current trends in the salerooms and current fashions, both here and overseas. But many antique dealers buy privately, and from each other, for prices which are less influenced by the volatile figures achieved at auction. Which is not to say that buying at auction is to be discouraged for private buyers. There are still good things to be bought in the salerooms, and for reasonable prices, providing the newcomer is prepared to tread warily and keep a cool head.

How to buy

The golden rule for buying antiques of any sort is to buy what you really like. It is you who will have to live with it, use it, clean it, polish it and show it off. Today, as in clothes, taste and fashion are eclectic and there is little point in owning something which makes you feel uncomfortable, however expensive or trendy it may be. If a teapot won't pour, don't buy it, however famous the maker. If the clock is exceptionally beautiful but its chimes are going to drive you mad, buy one a little less beautiful but which you can silence when you feel like it. If you can't sit at a dining room table because the chairs are too low or too high, even though they cost a King's ransom they aren't worth the price.

Above all, keep a sense of proportion. Compare the cost of a new canteen of silver with an old one by mixed makers and remember that ultimately you are buying knives and forks as well as silver. What would a brand new dinner service cost compared to a part service of Coalport or Derby? Or a set of dining chairs from a fashionable department store?

Introduction

Strange things happen to people's sense of values sometimes, and the actual purpose of an article seems to get forgotten in the heat of the moment. They become obsessed with the thought that they may have 'paid too much' for something, quite forgetting that the same object would probably cost twice as much brand new, if it could be found at all.

What to know

Some words hold a wealth of meaning, both in the trade and in the salerooms. They are used as a kind of shorthand and are not intended to deceive anyone, but, as in any other private vocabulary, outsiders often misunderstand the words, and regrettable mistakes may follow. Here are some of the most common: "Period" means 'of about the same date' as in "Chippendale period". "Style" means 'after the style of' and usually means a later copy or reproduction, as in "Adam style". "Chippendale" these days is used, as it is in America, to denote a particular style rather than as a direct attribution to the workshop of the man himself. The same applies to "Sheraton" and "Hepplewhite". "Georgian" is often used to describe a certain style as well as the period itself, and even when used as a form of dating is very loose and can mean any date for more than a hundred years, from 1714 to 1820. The same applies to "Queen Anne" as a description of style rather than period, particularly in the case of silver. "Provincial" is perhaps a slightly derogatory term when used for furniture, but a 'provincial' longcase clock or bracket clock denotes one of a particular design. In silver, 'provincial' may mean an assay office outside London, often rare, collectable and thus more expensive. "Sheffield Plate" or "Old Sheffield" means plated silver made from *c.*1740 by a special process. It should not be confused with the hallmark of the Sheffield Assay Office, which was in operation from *c.*1773 and prolific during the Victorian and Edwardian periods.

The descriptions to all the illustrations contain most of the technical terms in current use. When in doubt, use the glossary.

Where to buy

Antique dealers

Almost without exception, all established dealers are well qualified in their particular field, helpful, friendly and co-operative. Their prices are probably slightly higher than those in the salerooms, but like any other retailers, they have to cover their overheads and running costs, as well as giving you the benefit of years of experience, judgement and specialist knowledge. If there is anything that puzzles you, be it about price, period or quality, do not hesitate to ask. One vital question in every field should be 'Has it been restored?' or 'Do you know if it has been repaired?' Many dealers rescue wrecks from total extinction and, with the services of a qualified craftsman have the pieces restored to all their former glory. In these days of conservation, there is nothing wrong at all about such a practice – quite the contrary. But the dealer should tell his customers that it has been done.

Some dealers may have a notice "Trade only" in their windows. Private customers thinking to outsmart the dealer may find themselves with problems – anyone pretending to be 'trade' may well lose their legal protection as a private buyer or consumer. An antique shop is not a bazaar, and dealers dislike people who try and bargain with them without knowing what they are talking about. It is perfectly permissible to ask if the dealer will come down a little in his price, and if you show genuine enthusiasm for a particular piece they may well bring the price down just a bit, particularly if the object in question has been part of their stock for some time. But don't count on it.

Make certain you have a proper receipt for your purchase, stating clearly the total price paid, including VAT if applicable, and a full description of the piece which has been sold to you. The receipt will safeguard you against any possible errors on the part of the dealer and, providing you have good reason, allow you to return the article in the case of any errors you yourself have made.

Fairs and markets

These are fascinating places for the treasure-seeker and bargain hunter. Prices are usually lower than anywhere else, since the dealers have virtually no overheads, but the customer has little or no redress against any of the 'tricks of the trade'. As in all markets, there is likely to be a fair complement of 'fly-by-nights' among the genuine regulars, and it is a mistake to buy anything in a hurry. If you are serious about buying, spend some time just walking about, discovering who the 'regulars' are and who is unknown to the other dealers. If you see something you like, ask for a card giving the name and address of the dealer before even considering parting with your money. Most one or two-day fairs are put on by fair organisers who hold lists of names and addresses of all the dealers. The organiser's name is to be found displayed on posters and advertisements announcing the fair. In an open market you are on your own. Everyone has stories about finding wonderful things and everyone has stories about being taken for a ride.

It must be added that both in fairs and regular antique markets there are many stallholders who are extremely reputable and run small antique dealing businesses from their homes, travelling around fairs to find new customers. Many of them are only too happy if you suggest visiting them at their own addresses to see the rest of their stock.

Salerooms

Compared with the number of people who have ventured into antique shops or strolled down street markets, few people have been to an auction of any sort. Whether it is for farm machinery or wine or wholesale fruit and vegetables, all auctions are exciting, heady and unpredictable. And every auction house has a set of conditions of sale, setting out quite clearly all the details of the auction house's responsibilities. It cannot be repeated too often that *a saleroom is only acting as an agent for the seller*, and is in no way responsible for the condition or authenticity of anything which passes through their hands. This disclaimer is to be found in the conditions of sale of every variety of auction, not just those of antiques. It is essential, therefore, that the potential buyer reads these conditions of sale very carefully, and every time a different saleroom is visited, because the conditions vary. Check whether a buyer's commission is charged – many provincial salerooms have followed the big London auction rooms and charge a percentage which is added to the 'hammer price' plus VAT.

This varies, but it is usually between 8 per cent and 10 per cent. Payment must be made when stipulated – usually within 48 hours of the sale, and goods must be removed by the time stated – Phillips allow seven days, other auction houses may have a different time-limit. If the goods are not removed, the auctioneer has the right to resell them and charge you the costs of storage and the standard charges for selling the article.

Some salerooms simply print in their catalogues 'imperfections not stated', others that the absence of any description of damage does not imply that there are no defects and/or restoration. Frequently the only hint of poor condition or damage are the letters 'a.f.' meaning 'as found' and usually implying considerable damage. All Phillips' catalogues contain a short glossary of the code used in descriptions, and damage is usually fully described in the text, but they add that 'care is taken to ensure that any statement, e.g. as to maker, set number, description and condition is reliable and accurate, but all such statements are statements of opinion'.

All lots are available to be viewed before the sale – times of viewing are announced and printed in the catalogue. It is helpful when viewing to take into consideration the general standard and condition of everything else in the sale as well as the piece you may have your eye on. If the general standard is low and condition poor, look at your 'find' again. Read the descriptions carefully and check any coding for condition. There is a complete vocabulary for the description of antiques and if you do not understand any of the words, use the glossary at the back of this guide. It contains most of the words in current use in the categories the guide covers.

Estimates Where auction houses publish estimated prices, either at the end of each description in the catalogue or on a sheet displayed prominently on viewing day, check your price-limit against them, but remember that these can in no way be taken as a valuation of the object, only the amount the saleroom expects it to fetch on the day of the sale.

Reserves Most salerooms, including Phillips, state that all goods are put up for sale without reserve unless written instructions are received from the seller. These days it is rare for anything of any value to be sold without a reserve however. This is the price that the seller is prepared to accept for an object. If the bidding does not reach this figure it will be marked 'unsold' or 'bought in' in the auctioneer's book, although the auctioneers reserve the right to sell after the auction by private treaty after consultation with the seller. If yours was the last bid, but was below the reserve, you may ask the auctioneer after the sale if the seller is willing to accept your figure. No reserves are disclosed but are a confidential matter between the seller and the auctioneer. Unsold lots are not disclosed until after the sale.

Commission bids If you doubt your own nerve and would prefer not to bid yourself, or if for some reason you have attended the viewing and cannot attend the sale, make yourself known to a member of the auction room staff who will bid on your behalf. This is known as a 'commission bid' and accounts for an auctioneer's behaviour when he raises the bidding when there is apparently no one in the saleroom making any bids. As a further signal, if the commission bid seems to be the highest, the auctioneer will usually say 'With me, then, at . . .' and name the bid. When instructing someone to bid on your behalf it is a good idea to leave a little to his discretion. Remembering that you must add between 15 per cent and 25 per cent to the 'hammer price' for VAT and buyer's commission, give him your top figure, for the sake of argument say £200, but allow a couple more bids at his discretion, taking the 'hammer price' to £210 or £220. He will use those extra bids only if he feels they will secure the article for you.

Periods, dates and styles

Even when they are not being used to denote a style rather than a period, such as "Georgian", "Queen Anne" or "Adam" the naming of a period after a monarch does not mean precisely the dates of that monarch's reign. Changes were not abrupt but slow, gradually evolving from one style to another. Thus "William & Mary" runs from roughly 1690 to 1700, although William of Orange came to the throne in 1688 and reigned alone after the death of the Queen in 1694 until 1702. In metals and in pottery, this period is particularly important however and is precise: "William & Mary" 1688–1694 and "Williamite" 1694–1702. Again, Queen Anne's reign was remarkably short, a brief twelve years from 1702 to 1714 but it was an important period in terms of English style and changes in lifestyle and can often refer to a period almost ten years later, before the German lifestyle of the Hanoverian Georges filtered through from the Court to the upper and middle echelons of society. On page 14-16 there is a simple chart showing the main influences in change of style, use of material and naming the periods appropriately for each subject – there are slight variations in different fields – which can be used as a quick reference.

Country and provincial

The term "country furniture" is a relatively recent one, and denotes furniture made by country craftsmen, often in less expensive, more readily available woods. It is more simply made, often using traditional methods of construction, but following the general lines of the important cabinet makers and furniture makers of the period. Some examples of "country furniture" can be found on pages 90-91.

"Provincial" means different things in different fields, but in furniture particularly, it denotes furniture made, often to patterns by Chippendale, Hepplewhite and so on, but in provincial workshops, which often lagged behind "London" fashion by twenty years or more. Provincially-made furniture is sometimes more ostentatious and heavier in style than "London" furniture because provincial workshops wished to impress their clients with their expertise, and because their clients in turn wished to impress the local gentry with their newly acquired wealth. Once power-driven machinery was introduced into furniture-making and it began to be mass-produced in the provinces as well as in London, the difference was often even more marked, but from *c.*1880 there were no "country" versions of such fashionable articles as sofa tables, chiffoniers, and so on because they were being made cheaply enough in furniture factories and required techniques which only machines could achieve. Country craftsmen continued, however, to make traditional furniture such as gate-legged tables, Windsor chairs, dressers, corner cupboards, chests, and functional articles of every kind from the same traditional materials that had been used for centuries. The same is true for all the subjects covered in the guide – the advent of machine-made techniques did not obliterate the local potter, silversmith, clockmaker, cabinet-maker or craftsman. Indeed, many local skills were revived with the Arts & Crafts Movement in the 19th century, and many traditional shapes and forms were mass-produced during the Victorian and Edwardian periods.

A final word of warning on these products of "Tudor" and "Elizabethan" revivals. Great quantities of them were made, and now come within the legal definition of 'antique' i.e. a hundred years old or more. Many of them were finely made, by individual craftsmen and have in recent years acquired a high market value. But many of them were poor quality, made cheaply for the mass-market and of questionable design. With a little time and experience in handling antiques of all kinds, the difference will become obvious. Meanwhile it is as well to remember those trade words mentioned on page 11 and if in doubt the question "Can you be more precise about the date it was made?" can prove invaluable.

PERIOD	FURNITURE	CLOCKS	SILVER	POTTERY & PORCELAIN	GLASS
1660 1660 Fire of London **CAROLEAN** Charles II 1660–85 **1680**	OAK Christopher Wren Rebuilding of London 1666 Chinoiserie Inlay	1658 John Fromanteel Pendulum clocks London Longcase Clocks Verge Escapement Joseph Knibb 1640–1712	EARLY ENGLISH Dutch influence Christian Van Vianen d.1660 Chinoiserie	Tin Enamel Delft Fulham 1670 Blue & White Oriental	George Ravenscroft flint glass *c.*1670
James II 1685–8 **WILLIAM** **& MARY** 1658–94 **1700**	OAK WALNUT marquetry, parquetry Veneer Daniel Marot	Thomas Tompion 1639–1713	1685 Revocation of the Edict of Nantes Huguenot immigrants Jean Berain 1638–1711 Britannia Standard 1697	White Saltglaze *c.* 1684	
QUEEN **ANNE** 1702–14 **1730**	Grinling Gibbons 1648–1721 William Kent 1683–1748 WALNUT MAHOGANY	Anchor Escapement Provincial Longcase	QUEEN ANNE Paul de Lamerie 1688–1751 BAROQUE ROCOCO 1720	Liverpool *c.*1710 Meissen hard-paste porcelain *c.*1710	Methuen Treaty 1703 Port & Sherry 1713 German/Silesian glass imports Newcastle glass Engraved glass
George I 1714–27	Thomas Chippendale 1718–79 William Vile d.1767		1740 Sheffield Plate	Bow 1745–75 Chelsea 1745–69 Derby *c.*1749–1810	Stourbridge-Brierley Hill 1740 GLASS TAX 1745

EARLY GEORGIAN George II 1727–60 **1760**	Robert Adam 1728–1792 Gillows of Lancaster 1761–1906	Regulator clocks *c.*1752	Robert Adam *c.*1728–92 Robert Hennell 1763–1813 Hester Bateman 1761–90 ↓ CLASSICAL	Bow soft-paste porcelain *c.*1750 Wedgwood creamware *c.*1750 Worcester First Period *c.*1755–83	Enamelled glass Coloured glass Air-twists *c.*1755 Opaque Air-twists
George III 1760–1820 **LATE GEORGIAN** **1810**	George Hepplewhite d.1788 ↓ Thomas Shearer MAHOGANY SATINWOOD		↑ Boulton & Fothergill 1773–1809 Henry Chawner 1786–1810 ↓ REGENCY	Plymouth *c.*1770–1810 HARD-PASTE PORCELAIN *c.*1768 Bristol hard-paste Porcelain *c.*1770 Caughley *c.*1775–99 SOAPSTONE PORCELAIN Wedgwood pearlware *c.*1779 Masons ironstone *c.*1792 Minton *c.*1793 Spode bone china *c.*1794 Derby bone china *c.*1810	Waterford glass houses established *c.*1760 Cut glass chandeliers GLASS TAX DOUBLED 1776 Tax on enamelled glass *c.*1777 English glassmakers to Ireland 1780 Nailsea glass 1788 Heavy Waterford glass
1815 BATTLE OF TRAFALGAR George III 1760–1820 **REGENCY**	↑ Thomas Sheraton Thomas Hope 1770–1831 Brighton Pavilion 1817 Chinoiserie French Empire		↑ Paul Storr 1792–1838 Hunt & Roskell Rundell, Bridge, Rundell Brighton Pavilion 1817 Chinoiserie, French Empire	Nantgarw Swansea 1813–20 Doulton *c.*1815 Rockingham bone china *c.*1825	Graeco–Roman & classical Coloured glass Wall lights, chandeliers GLASS TAX–IRELAND 1825

	SATINWOOD		REGENCY		
George IV 1820–30 **1830**	Baroque Revival *c.*1820 'Abbotsford' Tudor & Jacobean (Sir Walter Scott)		Baroque Revival Emes & Barnard 1829		American press-moulded glass imports *c.*1825
WILLIAM IV 1830–37 Victoria 1837–1901 **EARLY VICTORIAN** 1851 Great Exhibition **1860**	Gothic Revival Medieval & Romantic OAK REVIVAL William Morris 1834–96	Skeleton clocks	Gothic Revival Electroplating 1840 Electrotyping Elkingtons 1843	Chamberlain's Worcester 1840–52	English press-moulded at Stourbridge, Newcastle *c.*1833 GLASS TAX LIFTED 1845 Iridescent glass Cameo glass
LATE VICTORIAN Victoria 1837–1901 **1900**	Arts & Crafts Movement Edward Ashbee 1863–1942 ART NOUVEAU E.W. Godwin 1833–86 Liberty & Co. 1875 C.F.A. Voysey 1857–1941	1880 Greenwich Meantime	Arts & Crafts Movement Japonaiserie ART NOUVEAU Acid Engraving, Acid etching *c.*1870	Royal Worcester 1862 Belleek 1863 ART NOUVEAU Lambeth Doulton Hannah Barlow	ART NOUVEAU Acid etching, engraving 1870 Gallé, 1846–1904 Daum 1853–1909 Thomas Webb Queens Burmese ware 1885
Edward VII 1901–10 George V 1910–36 1914 **EDWARDIAN** First World War 1918 **1920**	C.R. Mackintosh 1868–1928 'Glasgow School' Art Deco 1925			Martinware 1873–1915 William Moorcroft Macintyre 1897–1913	Aesthetic Movement Lalique 1860–1945 Tiffany 1848–1933

Furniture

Periods and styles

The shape, form and construction of antique furniture depends to a very great extent on the woods from which it is made, who used it, and for what purpose. Living conditions changed with the centuries, and whereas in Medieval and Tudor days there was very little furniture of any sort in all but the grandest houses, by the mid-18th century England had a prosperous middle-class living in well-built brick houses and the amount of furniture, its purpose and variety had grown enormously. From then until Victorian times, when rooms were over-furnished and cluttered with all manner of objects, social developments once again separated the rich from the poor, the well-endowed from the impoverished dweller in industrial towns with barely a stick of furniture to call his own.

Oak

This was the principal timber used in England for making furniture until the Restoration of Charles II in 1660. It is coarse-grained, splits easily and restricts shape and construction as well as moving and shrinking with time and atmospheric conditions. Mortise and tenon joints, panelled construction, chip carving and heavy relief carving, and turning on a lathe straight across the grain were the most suitable for oak. Heavy iron nails and steel strap hinges together with the limited number of tools used in those early days result in the typical chests, court cupboards, stools, tables, chairs and benches of the period sometimes known as the Age of Oak.

Walnut

After the Great Fire of 1666 London was almost completely rebuilt and the new houses with their multiplicity of rooms demanded a different sort of furniture from the old-fashioned high walls and timbered buildings. Twist-turning, marquetry, veneer and the use of walnut came into England from the Netherlands, first with the return of Charles II and then with William of Orange. The use and appearance of furniture changed radically: occasional chairs, chests with drawers, writing furniture and small tables furnished the neat new brickbuilt town houses and soon became fashionable all over England. Walnut is close-grained and will take both tight twist-turning and crisp detailed carving, as well as being able to be cut as a veneer. Oak could be twist-turned too, but it was difficult to achieve with the slow manpowered lathes, except on fairly thick timber which made it wasteful except for table legs and similar more heavy applications.

Veneer

Veneer is laid on a 'carcase' which is the completed piece of furniture made of cheaper wood, without decorative carving, beading or ornament. At first in England veneer was used on oak carcases but it was not satisfactory because of the movement of the timber which caused veneers to lift, as well as the coarse-grained nature of oak which did not provide a smooth enough surface, and soon deal, pine and softwood were substituted for carcases. Wonderful decorative effects were achieved with marquetry, parquetry and inlay, as well as the use of lacquer for grand cabinets and chests. At first panels were imported from the East and applied to carcases, but by the turn of the century English lacquer or 'japanning' had taken the place of foreign imports and 'chinoiserie' was in great demand. Beechwood was also used, either stained or painted, particularly for chairs, as well as some yew wood, cedar and elm for country furniture.

Mahogany

Soon architecture in England became influenced by classical Greek and Roman styles, first with William Kent, then the Palladian style, and finally by the Adams brothers. Furniture too took on architectural shapes, with pediments and cornices and 'double-heighted' bureaus, bureau bookcases and bureau cabinets to accord with the lofty size of rooms. The springy nature of walnut had enabled craftsmen to design and make a whole new range of furniture, particularly chairs and tables which had no need of stretchers between the legs to hold them firm, but which were based on the 'cabriole' leg cut from a single piece of timber and using the natural spring of the wood. When mahogany first came into England some time between 1720 and 1730 it was found to be an even more satisfactory wood for furniture-makers, both as a veneer and a solid timber. It was close-grained, immensely strong, and came in lengths and widths hitherto unknown due to the size and girth of the trees. Double-heighted furniture which had been made in two parts, could be made as a single unit because of the length and strength of mahogany. From Thomas Chippendale's vision of unity and concord in interior design grew the sleek classical lines of 18th-century furniture, making maximum use of beautiful undecorated surfaces in richly figured veneers. The carcases were also made in a cheaper mahogany, often called 'baywood' instead of pine and softwood.

Taste changed and Hepplewhite followed the fashion for lighter-coloured woods, a more delicate interpretation of classical themes, and less severe, more fluid lines. By the end of the 18th century, Sheraton in his turn had further lightened the lines of furniture, using cane, lattice, and tapering legs, as well as simulated bamboo and painted decoration, with an eye to the expanding market and the first large furniture manufacturers, many of whom made excellent use of his designs. Mass-produced brass screws, hinges and furniture fittings made it possible for all kinds of doors, lids, leaves and flaps to meet with minute hairline joins, giving the impression of sleek unbroken surfaces.

Machines

The Regency period was at once the apogee and turning point of some of the finest furniture made in England. But with the opulence and ostentation of a rich and successful nation, the pure classical forms were gradually adulterated. Brass inlay, brass marquetry, ormolu mounts and gilded wood embellished furniture of all kinds, and machines began to do the work of skilled craftsmen. When cut by hand, veneers are an eighth of an inch (30 mm) thick or more. Machines could cut them paper-thin, to one sixteenth of an inch (15mm) or even less. Handcut dovetail joints were chunky and longtailed – machines cut them shorter, stubbier and with mechanical precision. Turning on high-speed power-driven lathes allowed more coarse-grained woods to be used for more elaborate shapes, always mechanically symmetrical. When the Victorians began with nostalgia to reproduce early Tudor and Jacobean designs, with twist-turning and chip carving, the twists all turned the same way, the shallow machine carving bit into the grain where no hand-held chisel could make an impression without the wood splitting along the grain.

To these technical advances there were added every known variation in style and design, from Gothic to Regency revival, often mixed together with very questionable results. The Arts & Crafts Movement and Art Nouveau, both products of a reaction against the tasteless clutter of Victorian interiors, did much to revive the genuine art of the craftsman in England and indeed had repercussions on interior design throughout Europe, and in America.

Principal woods used in furniture-making and their purposes

Woods have different characteristics as well as colours and grains. Early woodworkers used woods most suitable for their purposes, because the wood itself dictated how it could be worked and the speed of man-powered lathes limited the amount of turning, carving and cutting. Machine tools can cut, turn and shape timber regardless of the nature and grain of the wood. This is a fundamental clue to the authenticity of antique furniture. *Note:* Country furniture is always in solid wood and never veneered.

Solid woods

Ash chairs, chair legs, 17th and 18th century.

Beech chairs, particularly twist-turned, 17th and 18th century.

Birch chairs 17th to 19th century.

Cedar 16th to 19th century and as cabinet fittings 18th century.

Chestnut some English country, but mainly continental.

Coromandel small items, 19th century.

Deal, Pine carcase wood 17th and 18th century. Cheap domestic furniture 19th century.

Elm chair seats, Windsors, 16th to 19th century. With oak in country furniture.

Fruitwood (apple, pear, plum) Country furniture to 18th century.

Mahogany Hispaniola from c.1730, Honduras from *c.*1750 and as carcase wood 18th and 19th century, known as 'baywood'. African in 19th century.

Maple underframes for chairs, 18th and 19th century.
Oak all periods, country, and as drawer linings and cabinet fittings 18th and 19th century. Unseasoned as carcase in some 19th century.
Padouk often Dutch or Continental, mid-18th and English 19th century.
Pine, Deal carcase wood 17th and 18th century. Domestic furniture 18th and 19th century.
Plane chairs, underframes, fly brackets, 18th and 19th century.
Rosewood as veneer from mid-18th century, solid in 19th century.
Satinwood as solid from *c.*1780, from 19th century as a veneer.
Teak rare before 19th century then quite popular.
Walnut rich brown native English, and French to 1720. Virginia 'red walnut' (unpolished) from late 17th century. Machine cut polished (black) and unpolished from *c.*1830.
Yew wood Highly prized. Country furniture, particularly hoops on Windsors 16th–19th century.

Principal veneers
Amboyna 18th and 19th century.
Birch or Satinbirch 19th century.
Burr Walnut (also burr elm etc. meaning the root) 17th and 18th century.
Chestnut some use as substitute for satinwood late 18th and 19th century.
Coromandel 19th century.
Harewood (stained sycamore) 18th century.
Kingwood 18th and 19th century.
Laburnum 18th and 19th century.
Mahogany Hispaniola to *c.*1750, San Domingo and Cuban from *c.*1750. All varieties 19th century.
Maple stained, 18th century, 'birds' eye' 19th century.
Olive oyster veneer, parquetry, 17th and early 18th century.
Partridge 18th and 19th century.
Plum up to late 17th century.
Rosewood as veneer late 18th century. Solid, 19th century.
Satinwood as solid from *c.*1780, from 19th century as veneer.
Sycamore stained, known as 'harewood'.
Tulipwood from *c.*1780.
Walnut native English and French from late 17th and early 18th century.
Yew wood parquetry in 17th century, veneer in 18th century.
Zebrawood late 18th century and some 19th century.

Stringing, inlay and crossbanding
Boxwood 16th to 18th century.
Coromandel late 18th century.
Ebony late 17th–19th century.
Holly late 16th–18th century.
Kingwood 18th and 19th century.
Mahogany 18th and 19th century.
Olive late 17th and early 18th century.
Satinwood late 18th century.
Tulipwood from *c.*1780.
Walnut late 17th century and early 18th century.
Yew wood 18th century.
Zebrawood late 18th century.

A Carolean decorated oak open armchair with cane panel back and pierced scroll cresting. Pair £600–900.

Principal furniture designers and cabinet-makers

Adam, Robert 1728–92. Second and best-known son of William Adam, Scottish architect.

Ashbee, C.R. 1863-1942. Founded Guild & School of Handicrafts. 1888.

Chippendale, Thomas *c.*1718–79. *The Gentleman & Cabinet Maker's Directory* published first edition 1754.

Eastlake, C.L. 1836–1906. *Hints on Household Taste in Furniture* first published 1868.

Gibbons, Grinling 1648–1721. Wood carver and designer, worked with Christopher Wren.

Gillow, Richard 1734–1811. Son, Richard 1773–1849. Firm of Gillows established 1761–1906.

Godwin, E.W. 1833–86. Architect, designer, textile and wallpaper designer, strongly influenced by Japanese.

Hepplewhite, George *d.*1786. *Cabinet Maker & Upholsterers' Guide* published posthumously 1788.

Heal, Sir Ambrose 1872–1959. Furniture designer, founder of progressive furnishing store, greatly influenced by William Morris, Ernest Gimson, Arts & Crafts Movement.

Hope, Thomas 1770–1831. Seminal influence in grand Regency design.

Ince, William. In parnership with John Mayhew. *The Universal System of Household Furniture* by Ince & Mayhew published 1760.

Kent, William 1685–1748. Architect and interior designer.

Linnell, John. Upholsterer and cabinet-maker working from *c.*1761. *d.*1796.

Manwaring, Robert. Chair-maker and designer. *The Cabinet and Chair-Maker's Real Friend and Companion* published 1765.

Marot, Daniel 1662–1752. Early Continental influence on English furniture.

Mackintosh, Charles Rennie 1868–1928. Breakaway furniture designer from the Glasgow school influential in Art Nouveau.

Mayhew, John. See Ince.

Morris, William 1834–96. Founder of Arts & Crafts Movement and craftsman revival.

Seddon, George 1727–1801. Cabinet-maker, member of the Joiner's Company, and Master in 1795.

Shearer, Thomas. Cabinet-maker, artist of many plates in *Cabinet Maker's Book of Prices* published 1788.

Sheraton, Thomas. *Cabinet Maker and Upholsterers' Drawing Book* published in 1791–94. *Cabinet Dictionary* published 1803.

Vile, William. Partner with John Cobb and cabinet-maker to George III. *d.*1767.

Voysey, C.F.A. 1857–1941. Important designer of Art Nouveau furniture.

Late 17th-century oak 'Derbyshire' chair with applied turned decoration and carved panel back. £2000–3000.

A 17th-century oak panel-back chair with scroll arms, arcaded frieze to seat and turned arm supports. £1500–2000.

A 19th-century oak 'Derbyshire' chair with arms terminating in grotesque heads and foliate carved decoration. Pairs: £1000–1500.

Charles II twist-turned chairs in walnut with caned back and seat and raised front rail. Set of 4: £2400–3800.

One of a set of eight oak Carolean-style open-arm chairs with turned pillar back supports, scroll carved legs and scroll arms.
Set of 8: £1800–3000.

Ornately carved high-backed chairs in the style of Daniel Marot with carved centre stretcher, scroll legs and hoof feet with stuffover seat.
Set of 6: £4000–6000.

Wing chairs

Charles II carved walnut high-backed chair with Braganza scroll arm supports, carved scrolling front legs and turned stretchers. £3000–4000.

Wing chair in William & Mary taste with walnut frame, turned stretchers and outward-curving arms with typically rigid Victorian lines. £800–1200.

Queen Anne wing chair with walnut frame, outward-curving back legs and pad feet with flowing lines and outward-curving generous arms. £4000–6000.

Wing chairs

George I wing chair with cabriole legs with carved scallop knee decoration and pad feet, flowing shape and outward-curving arms. £3000–4000.

George II 'Gainsborough' chair in carved mahogany with pierced fret decoration to spandrels and stretchers and carved curving arms. £4000–6000.

Regency rosewood bergere with cut-brass inlay and cane back with sabre-shaped legs. £1500–2000.

George II tub chair in bergere style with carved mahogany frame edged with brass studs and tapered square legs. £1500–2000.

Queen Anne walnut dining chair with heavy seat frieze, cabriole legs, pad feet and single back stretcher.
Set of 8: £8000–12000.

Queen Anne walnut dining chair with curved seat, turned stretchers and plain cabriole legs.
Set of 8: £10000–15000.

George I dining chair with square seat frame, shallow-carved decoration to knees of cabriole legs and plain stout stretchers.
Set of 6: £6000–8000.

George II plain mahogany dining chair with raised front stretcher, straight back splat and stuffover square seat.
Set of 6: £2000–3000.

George II mahogany dining chair with elaborately-carved shell decoration to knees of cabriole legs, ball-and-claw feet and decorative back splat. Set of 6: £6000–8000.

George II carved mahogany dining chair with ornate cabriole legs, raised decorative crest rail and curved back with pierced and carved back splat. Set of 8: £10 000–15 000.

Carved mahogany dining chair from the Chippendale period with ornately-carved cabriole legs, ball-and-claw feet and over-running upward-curving crest rail. Set of 6: £6000–8000.

A 19th-century, carved mahogany, dining chair in the Chippendale taste with plain cabriole legs and pad feet with 'ribbon' style back. Set of 8: £2000–3000.

George III mahogany elbow chair in the Chippendale manner with S-scroll arms, square chamfered legs and decorative back. Pairs: £2000.

Carved mahogany chair in Chippendale style with Gothic vase back splat and plain chamfered legs. Set of 6: £6000–8000.

George III arm chair in the Chinese taste with 'cracked ice' back and cane seat, plain chamfered legs and decorative spandrels. Pairs: £2000–2500.

George III carved mahogany chair in the Chinese taste with 'pagoda' crest rail and plain chamfered legs.
Set of 4: £3000–4000.

Early lyre-backed chair with Chippendale characteristics, tapered square-sectioned legs on castors and S-scroll arms. Set of 4: £2000–3000.

Round-backed chair with serpentine curve to the front seat rail, outward-curving back legs and fluted tapered square-sectioned legs. Set of 6: £2000–3000.

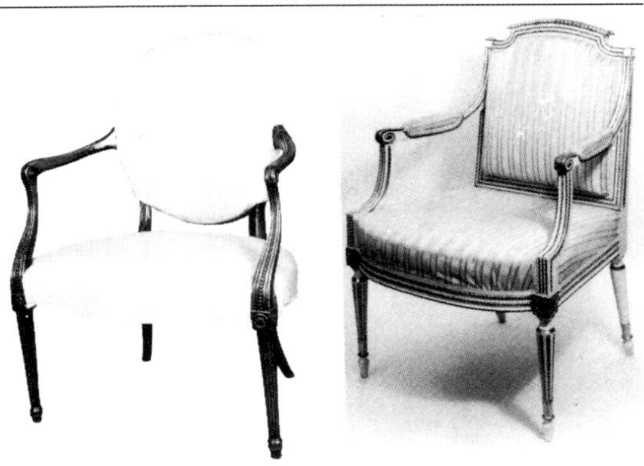

George III open-armed chair with stuffover back, outward-curving arms with beaded decoration and turned tapered front legs. Pairs: £3000–4000.

Regency open-armed chair in painted and gilded beechwood with square back, raised crest rail, curved arms and elegant turned tapered legs on peg feet. Pairs: £4000–6000.

George III elbow chair in the French taste with carved frieze rail and knees, curved front legs and French scroll feet. £2000–3000.

George III mahogany chair of Hepplewhite shield-back design with dished seat, square tapering legs and plain stretchers. Set of 6: £3000–4000.

George III carved mahogany chair in Hepplewhite style with shield back, stuffover seat, tapering square-sectioned legs with peg feet and plain stretchers. Set of 4: £1500–2000.

Ornate version of the shield back, with downward-curving open arms, curvaceous back and turned tapering front legs. Set of 4: £6000–8000.

Early 19th-century ebonised chair of shield-back design with painted decoration, Prince of Wales feathers back, downward-curving arms, stuffover seat and square-sectioned tapering legs. Pair: £6000–8000.

George III chairs in Sheraton style with carved mahogany square back, stuffover seat and tapering reeded legs. Set of 6: £4000–6000.

Plain provincial chair in Sheraton style with stuffover seat, reeded decoration to back uprights and tapering square-sectioned reeded legs. Set of 6: £3000–4000.

Carved mahogany dining chair of simple design with swagged carved back, leather seat of broad proportions, square tapering legs and plain stretchers. Set of 6: £3000–4000.

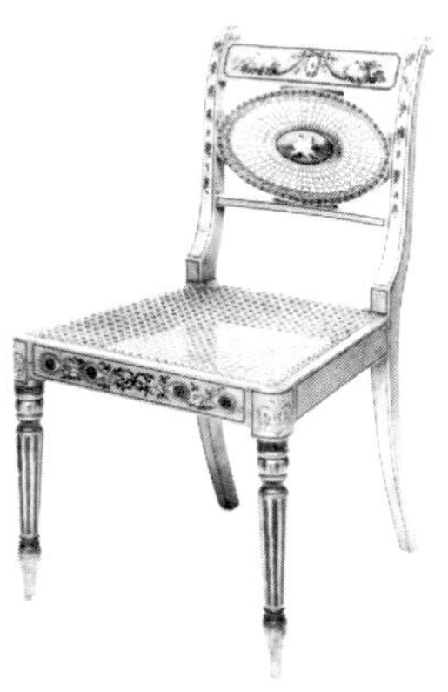

Painted satinwood chair with peacocks' eye and floral decoration, oval caned panel-back, cane seat and turned and tapered front legs with peg feet. Pairs: £1000–1500.

'Windsor'

An early 19th-century yew-wood and elm Windsor Elbow chair with pierced vase splat and stick uprights. £800–1200.

George III yew wood Windsor arm chair with Gothic pointed back, cabriole legs, dished seat and 'cows' horn' stretcher. £2000–3000.

Late 18th-century yew wood and elm Windsor chair with saddle seat, turned legs and 'cows' horn' stretcher. £800–1200.

Regency mahogany dining chair with sabre leg, upholstered seat and rope-twist back. Set of 6: £3000–4000.

Regency carved mahogany dining chair with S-curved arm, carved scrolled sabre leg and scrolled crest rail. Pairs: £3000.

Above Matching single carved mahogany dining chair with scrolled sabre legs and foliate carving and scrolled crest rail. Set of 6: £3000.

Right Regency mahogany dining chair with rosewood-panelled bar top rail, flush sides and sabre legs with drop-in seat. Set of 6: £3000–4000.

Left Plain balloon-back chair with upholstered seat and square seat frame, with turned and tapering front legs. Set of 6: £800–1200.

Above right A 19th-century mahogany dining chair with stuffover seat, reeded carving to back uprights and turned and tapering legs. Set of 6: £1500–2000.

Ebonized dining chair designed by Bruce Talbert and made by Gillows, bearing their stamp, with bobbin-turned back and reel-turned and carved front legs with taper-turned stretchers. Set of 8: £800–1200.

Dining chair in walnut with drop-in seat, square, chamfered legs and slightly curving back, designed by Ambrose Heal. Set of 6: £600–800.

Bentwood chair in laminated wood, probably birch, of a standard design after the original concept by Michael Thonet. Cane seat, splayed back legs and hooped back in one continuous curve, with circular hoop below seat frame. £200–250 for standard design in good condition.

Lloyd Loom armchair or easy chair in basket work with curved back, straight seat, turned cross-stretchers and legs bound with cane terminating in clamped metal feet. Painted in apple green, sprayed with gold finish. £100–150.

A 17th-century oak refectory table with turned legs, floor-level stretchers, two plank width, with minimal decoration on the frieze and small shaped spandrels. 7 ft/2.10 m long. £3000–4000.

Below Late 17th-century oak refectory table with chip-carved frieze in geometric and tulip design, with curved shaped spandrels and baluster-turned legs and low square stretchers. 8 ft/2.44 m long. £6000–8000.

Early Dutch oak draw-leaf table with bulb-shaped legs with low flat stretcher and grooved corner decoration to the frieze. £1500. If English: £4000–6000.

Early 17th-century oak credence table with octagonal folding top, simple turned legs and solid pegged stretchers, with a gate support pivoting from the back. 29 in/74.8 cm. £1050. If English: £2600–3500.

An 18th-century yew wood gate-legged table with central drawer in the frieze, baluster-turned decoration to the plain square legs, small bun feet, and simple shaped frieze. 6½ ft/1.98 m. Rare £8000–12 000. In oak £2000–3000.

George III mahogany spider-legged table with fine reel and bobbin-turned legs, and two gate supports to either leaf. 3 ft 6 in/1.07 m. £1000–1500.

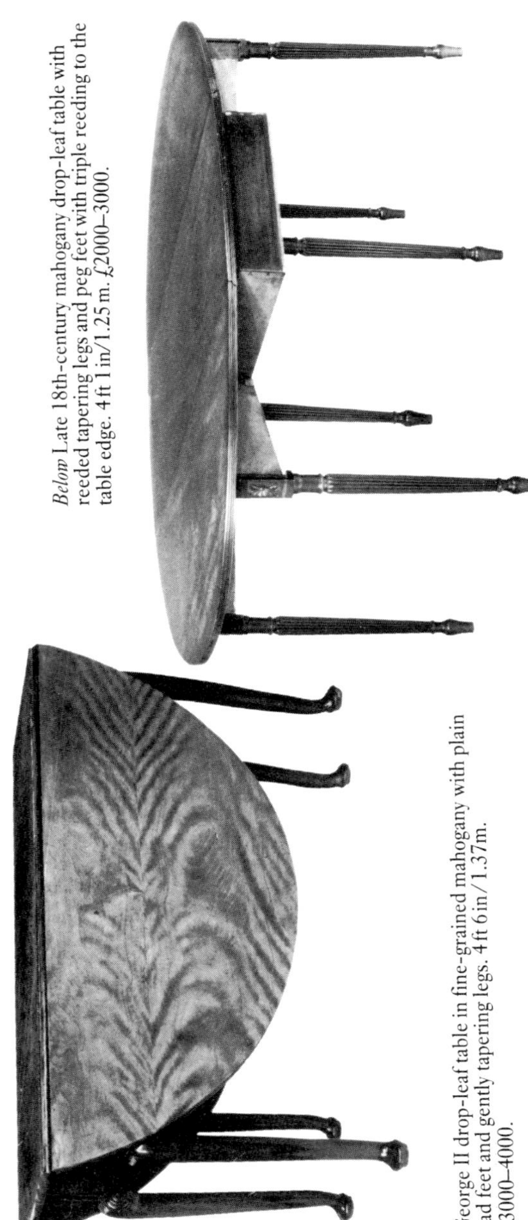

Below Late 18th-century mahogany drop-leaf table with reeded tapering legs and peg feet with triple reeding to the table edge. 4 ft 1 in/1.25 m. £2000–3000.

George II drop-leaf table in fine-grained mahogany with plain pad feet and gently tapering legs. 4 ft 6 in/1.37m. £3000–4000.

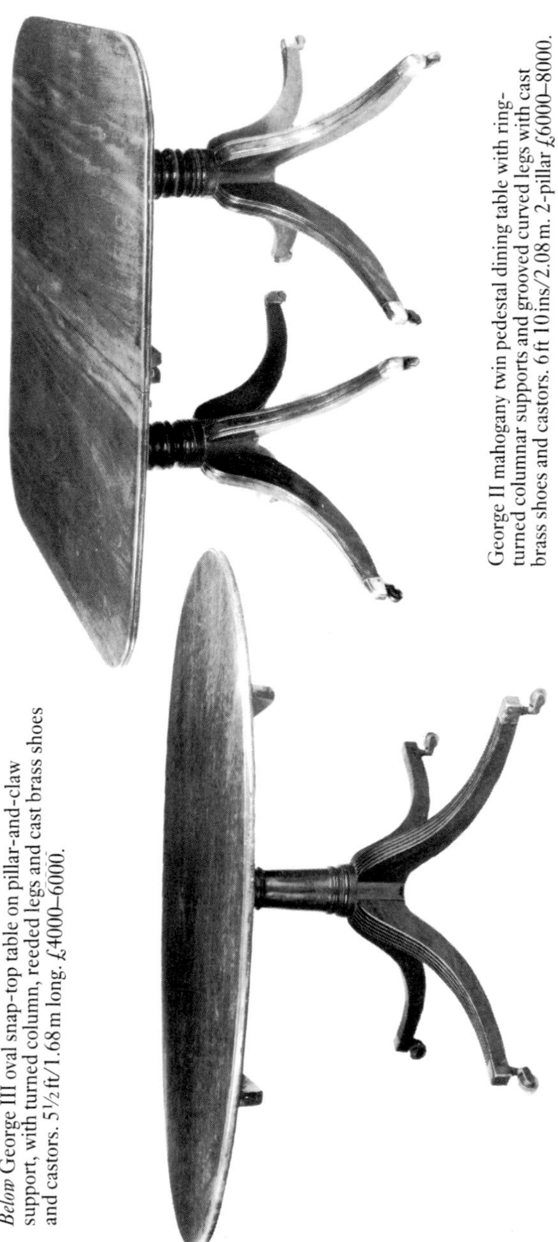

George II mahogany twin pedestal dining table with ring-turned columnar supports and grooved curved legs with cast brass shoes and castors. 6 ft 10 ins/2.08 m. 2-pillar £6000–8000.

Below George III oval snap-top table on pillar-and-claw support, with turned column, reeded legs and cast brass shoes and castors. $5\frac{1}{2}$ ft/1.68 m long. £4000–6000.

Early Victorian mahogany dining table with six concentric leaves on pull-out supports with simulated bamboo stretchers and applied ornament above round bun feet. £6000–8000.

Above George III snap-top oval table with ring-turned tapering columnar support and reeded legs with cast brass shoes and castors. 6 ft/1.80 m long. £5000–8000.

Regency rosewood circular snap-top table, cross-banded in yew wood on pillar-and-claw support with cast brass paw feet and castors. 3 ft/91 cm. £3000–4000.

Regency rosewood snap-top circular supper table with cut brass inlay on central plinth terminating in four splayed feet with cast brass paw feet and castors. 3 ft/91 cm. £6000–8000.

Regency kingwood breakfast table with snap top, cross-banded in satinwood with reeded edge on four slender pillars and plinth terminating in satinwood and ebony inlaid curving feet with cast brass paw feet and castors. 4 ft 2 in / 1.28 m. £3000–4000.

Regency rosewood snap-top breakfast table, inlaid with brass stringing on four slender columns and plinth terminating in scrolled curving legs and cast brass lion's mask feet and castors. 47 in/120 cm. £2500–3000.

George III library table inset with brown leather on tapering square-sectioned legs, brass shoes and castors, with two drawers in the frieze matched by two dummy drawers on the opposite side. 4 ft 2 in/1.28 m. £2000–3000.

Regency mahogany writing table with pierced brass gallery, on turned and reeded tapering legs, peg feet, brass shoes and castors, with two frieze drawers with lion's mask and ring handles. 3 ft 6 in/1.07 m. £3000–4000.

Regency mahogany library table inset with green leather with Greek key banding, on turned and tapering legs, with three frieze drawers and dummy drawers alternating on the sides. 5 ft 10 in/1.77 m. £3000.

Small-sized Regency writing table with concave central frieze drawer and two pairs of drawers on either side, plain wooden gallery and turned and reeded tapering legs. 3 ft 2 in / 98 cm. £1000–1500.

Small-sized Regency mahogany drum-top library table in rosewood, inset with leather and boxwood stringing, on turned column and tripod legs, with alternate drawers and dummy drawers in the frieze. 2 ft 10 in/90 cm diameter. £3000–4000.

Below Regency mahogany drum-top library table with eight drawers in the frieze, inset with tooled leather and boxwood stringing, on pillar support and four splayed legs with brass shoes and castors. 4 ft 4 in/1.32 m. £4000–6000.

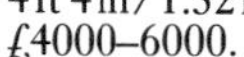

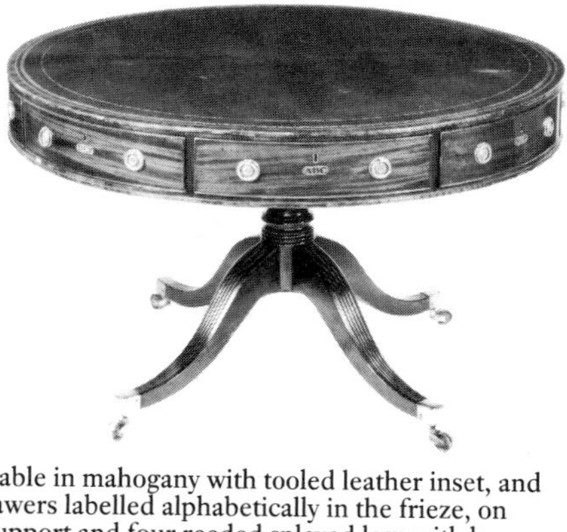

Regency rent table in mahogany with tooled leather inset, and eight frieze drawers labelled alphabetically in the frieze, on central pillar support and four reeded splayed legs with brass shoes and castors. 3 ft 7 in/1.09 m. £8000–12 000.

Left Regency mahogany and satinwood sofa table with boxwood and ebony stringing with one drawer and one dummy drawer on either side, one fitted with easel writing flap. 4 ft 11 in/1.50 m. £6000–8000.

Right Lyre-ended sofa table with applied anthemion ornament in rosewood and brass stringing with two drawers in the frieze on curved bracket feet with brass shoes and castors. £3000–4000.

Above Sofa table in rosewood and satinwood of Sheraton design, cross-banded in satin birch with two drawers and two dummy drawers in the frieze, on slender turned columns and splayed legs with brass shoes and castors. £6000–8000.

George II card table in red walnut and mahogany with shell-carved knees to the bold cabriole legs, terminating in ball-and-claw feet, with one drawer in the frieze and recesses for counters on the playing surface. 2 ft 11 in/89 cm. £3000–4000.

Mid-18th-century card and games table with flush drawer in the frieze, with shell decoration to the knees of the slender cabriole legs, tapering to hoofed feet. 3 ft/91.5 cm. £2500–3000.

George III mahogany serpentine card table in Hepplewhite taste with canted corners and tapering square-sectioned legs. 2 ft 7 in/79 cm. Pair: £8000–12 000.

Regency rosewood games table with hinged sliding top concealing a panel for chess, the drawer beneath inlaid for backgammon, on ring-turned column and reeded, hipped, splayed legs, with decorative brass shoes and castors. 2 ft/62 cm closed. £4000–6000.

Below Victorian demilune games table veneered in burr walnut with carved acanthus-leaf base to pillar and vineleaf decoration to the scrolled curving legs. 3 ft/91.5 cm. £1000–1500.

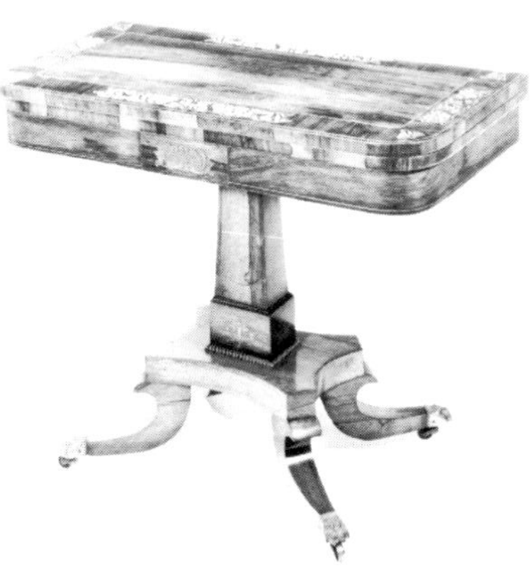

Regency rosewood and brass marquetry card table with D-shaped hinged top and anthemion decoration to the frieze and base of rectangular beaded pillar, on curved splayed legs below a central plinth, terminating in brass paw feet and castors. 2 ft 7 in/78.5 cm. Pair: £6000–8000.

Mid-18th-century serpentine card table with anthemion decoration to the frieze and curving legs, terminating in French scroll feet. 2 ft 7 in/79 cm. Pair: £8000–12 000.

Partridge and satinwood games table with central panel for chess sliding out to disclose a backgammon board, on fine tapered legs with cross-stretchers. 3 ft 2 in / 97 cm. £3000–4000.

George III silver table in the Chippendale manner with Chinese lattice gallery and decorative frieze, on cluster column legs with block feet and castors. 2 ft 5 in/73.5 cm. £8000–12 000.

George III mahogany dumb waiter on tripod stand, the three tiers with reeded moulded edging and the central pillar turned with swirling knop decoration. £1000–1500.

Regency plate and cutlery stand with spindle-turned gallery and ring-turned legs with brass shoes and castors. £2000–3000.

Early 19th-century set of four quartetto tables in amboyna with boxwood stringing on straight-turned legs. £2000.

George III burr yew wood and satinwood Pembroke table cross-banded in tulipwood with single frieze drawer and square tapering legs. 2 ft 8 in/81.5 cm. £4000–6000.

George III harlequin Pembroke table with satinwood cross-banding and rising top with two dummy drawers to conceal the well, and two matching small drawers, on slender, tapering legs. £6000–8000.

George III mahogany Pembroke table inlaid with harewood with a satinwood centre panel with floral inlay, cross-banded in rosewood and inlaid with husks and foliage, opening to form an oval table. £6000–8000.

George III Pembroke table in sycamore veneer with mahogany cross-banding with an inlaid marquetry conch shell opening to form an oval table. £6000–8000.

George III demilune side table in sycamore veneer with mahogany cross-banding and inlaid marquetry conch shell and slender tapering legs on block feet. 2 ft 8 in/81.5 cm. £2000–3000.

Below George III satin birch and mahogany demilune table with scallop-edged cross-banding and boxwood stringing with sunray veneer on square tapering legs and collared feet. £2000–3000.

George III satinwood demilune with inlaid husk and foliage and ebony stringing with decorative paterae on the frieze and inlaid, square tapering legs with block feet. £2800–3000.

One of a pair of early 19th-century papier-mâché and gilt heightened occasional tables, with a rectangular top, trefoil platform and scroll feet. Pair: £1000–1500.

A 19th-century satinwood and painted centre table with swags and flowerheads encircling a central panel depicting a muse or goddess, shaped frieze and curved legs with French scroll feet and a small circular undertier. £600–1000.

William and Mary laburnum and walnut cabinet with oyster veneer and boxwood stringing, a cushion drawer below the cornice, the stand with one long frieze drawer and twist-turned legs with flat stretchers. The interior is fitted with small drawers 3 ft 2 in/96 cm wide. £6000–8000.

William and Mary chest on stand with quarter-veneered doors strung with boxwood, a cushion drawer below the cornice, the stand with a single frieze drawer and twist-turned legs with flat stretchers and bun feet. 3 ft 6 in/1.07 m wide. £5000–7000.

George I walnut secretaire cabinet in two parts, with seaweed-marquetry panels and fitted fallfront secretaire drawer, above two short and two long drawers, on plain small bun feet. 7 ft 6 in/2.29 m high, 3 ft 2 in/96.5 cm wide. £6000–8000.

George II burr walnut secretaire with concave lunette in the base drawer inlaid with radial sunburst, the panelled doors concealing fitted pigeonholes and drawers. 7 ft 8 in/2.34 m high, 4 ft 1 in/1.25 m wide. £8000–12 000.

Queen Anne walnut bureau-cabinet with broken-arched pediment and arched mirrored doors concealing fitted drawers and pigeonholes, with one long dummy drawer concealing the inner well, above two short and two long drawers with brass mounts and handles, on plain bracket feet. 7 ft 8 in/2.34 m high, 3 ft 2 in/97 cm wide. £15 000–20 000.

Queen Anne lacquered bureau-cabinet with double arched moulded pediment and mirror doors concealing fitted drawers and pigeonholes with a 'secret' drawer in each arch, and a well beneath the interior writing surface, above a pair of short drawers and two long drawers. 7 ft 2 in/2.18 m high, 3 ft 8 in/112 cm wide. £20 000–30 000.

Queen Anne walnut bureau-cabinet with undulating arched pediment and arched mirrored doors, the interior fitted with flights of small drawers and compartments, and below the slope front a well above four shallow drawers with drop handles, on bracket feet. 7 ft 6 in/2.07 m high, 3 ft 6 in/1.07 m wide. £20 000–30 000.

Bureau-cabinet

Early 18th-century walnut bureau-cabinet with block-fronted doors concealing a fitted interior, above the slope front, with fluted columns on either side of three graduated drawers, on plain bun feet. 7 ft 2 in / 2.18 m high, 3 ft 3 in / 99 cm wide. £8 000–12 000.

George II mahogany and burr yew wood secretaire cabinet in the manner of William Hallett with carved acanthus foliage decoration to the cornice and chamfered sides, on bracket feet. 7 ft 8 in/2.34 m high, 3 ft 10 in/1.17 m wide. £10 000–15 000.

Chippendale period bureau-bookcase in mahogany with broken pediment, glazed doors with astragal moulding in star pattern, with an interior well concealed by two dummy drawers above three long graduated drawers, on bracket feet.
7 ft 1 in / 2.16 m high,
3 ft 3 in / 99.5 cm wide.
£10 000–15 000.

George III secretaire bookcase in satinwood and tulipwood with boxwood and ebony stringing, with applied decoration to the broken swan-neck pediment, dentil cornice, glazed doors with astragal moulding, the fallfront concealed by two cockbeaded dummy drawers above three graduated drawers, with narrow shaped apron and splayed feet.
7 ft 4 in/2.23 m high,
3 ft 5 in / 1.06 m wide.
£10 000–15 000.

George III mahogany secretaire bookcase with swan-necked pediment and Gothic glazing bars to the doors and fielded panel doors below the fallfront concealing document drawers, on bracket feet.
7 ft 1 in/2.16 m high,
3 ft 5 in/1.06 m wide.
£5000–7000.

Late 19th-century mahogany and satinwood cross-banded secretaire bookcase with geometrical glazing bars and three graduated drawers, on splayed bracket feet.
7 ft 2 in/2.18 m high,
3 ft 4 in/1.02 m wide.
£5000–7000.

George III mahogany secretaire cross-banded with tulipwood, with swan neck pediment and dentil cornice with Gothic glazing bars to the doors, and three graduated drawers below the fallfront, on ogee bracket feet.
6 ft 6 in/1.98 cm high,
3 ft/91.5 cm wide.
£6000–8000.

Queen Anne walnut bureau, the slope front quarter-veneered and cross-banded, with fitted interior and interior well concealed by a dummy drawer flanked by pull-out supports or lopers, above three graduated drawers, on bracket feet. 3 ft 3 in/99 cm high, 3 ft/91.5 cm wide. £4000–6000.

William and Mary oak bureau with split mouldings, the sloping fall with a book ledge enclosing a fitted graduated interior with drawers of concave outline, pigeonholes and well with sliding compartment with wrought iron clasp containing two short and two long drawers, on bracket feet. £1600–2200.

George III mahogany bureau with boxwood stringing and an interior well flanked by pull-out supports above two short and two long graduated drawers, on bracket feet. 3 ft 2 in / 97 cm high, 3 ft 1 in/94 cm wide. £3000–4000.

George III mahogany bureau with brass mounted bail handles and escutcheons, the interior well concealed by a single dummy drawer above a flight of three graduated drawers, on carved ogee bracket feet. 3 ft 3 in / 99.5 cm high, 3 ft / 91.5 cm wide. £2000–3000.

George III mahogany architects' table with boxwood stringing and double-ratcheted hinged top inset with leather, with three frieze drawers matched by three dummy drawers on the opposite side. 3 ft/91.5 cm wide. £3000–4000.

George III partners' pedestal desk in mahogany with tooled leather-inset top, three drawers of equal width in the frieze, and two flights of three graduated drawers on either side. 5 ft 2 in/1.57 m wide. £6000–8000.

A 19th-century partners' desk with rounded corners on flush pedestal base and reeded edge to the leather-inset top, with three drawers of equal width in the frieze and two flights of graduated drawers on either side, fitted with Bramah locks. £4000–6000.

Below A 19th-century mahogany partners' pedestal desk with turned wooden handles, thumb-moulded edge to the leather-inset top, and two doors below concealing document drawers. £3000–4000.

Victorian davenport in walnut, cross-banded, with boxwood stringing and inlaid decorative medallions of anthemion, with four drawers with turned wooden handles in the side, and matching dummy drawers on the other side.
2 ft 9 in/84 cm high, 1 ft 9 in/53.5 cm wide. £800–1200.

Victorian davenport in walnut, cross-banded with thuyawood and with boxwood stringing, the top with pierced brass gallery, pull-out fitted writing drawer and four drawers in the base concealed by a flush-fitting door. 3 ft/91.5 cm high, 1 ft 9 in/53.5 cm wide. £1600–2200.

A 19th-century, small-sized, roll-top or tambour-topped ladies' writing table, with fitted interior and fitted writing drawer in the frieze, on square tapering legs and castors. 3 ft 1 in/94 cm wide. £3000–4000.

Late 19th-century kingwood and parquetry desk with gilt mounts and ornate gilt metal candleholders, in the manner of a small Carlton House desk, with curved fitted drawers, leather-topped writing surface and two drawers in the frieze, on curved tapering legs with gilt metal acanthus and paw feet. 3 ft 5 in/1.04 m wide. £2500–3500.

Late Georgian satinwood and tulipwood cross-banded sheveret with oval mahogany-veneered panels to two small doors concealing drawers and pigeonholes, with hinged baize-lined writing surface above a single flush-fitting frieze drawer. £1500–2500.

George III mahogany sheveret with undulating curved superstructure, the three central drawers flanked by flush-fitting doors concealing drawers, with hinged baize-lined writing top on square tapering legs and peg feet. £2000–3000.

Late Georgian satinwood and tulipwood bonheur du jour with swan neck pediment, inlaid chequerwork and small decorative medallions, on square tapering gaitered legs. £3000–4000.

George III mahogany bonheur du jour or ladies' work table with simple lines, hinged baize-lined writing surface with two pull-out supports, with turned bone handles, on square tapering legs. £1500–2000.

A 16th-century oak coffer of frame and panel construction with coffered panelled lid with iron hinges and fastening, iron carrying-handles and simple geometric carving on the front panels. 4 ft 9 in/1.44 m wide. £2000–3000.

Oak coffer of 17th-century ark type with ridged lid and iron strap hinges and fastening, of basic frame and panel construction with mortise and tenon joints, iron carrying-handles and shallow decorative carving on the front panels. 4 ft 3 in/1.30 m wide. £2000–3000.

Massive Victorian stained-oak coffer of a type similar to Italian '*cassone*' with mock-Tudor relief decoration and romantic medieval figures, with lion's mask carving and brass ring handles. £1000–1500.

A 15th-century aumbry or livery cupboard, often no more than oak doors set in the wall, with pierced Gothic decoration, iron cockshead hinges, probably made up later as a cupboard. £3000–5000.

Late 16th-century carved oak court cupboard with stylised tulip and scroll strapwork, reel-turned columns and guilloche frieze. £3000–4000.

Late 17th-century oak side table with turned wooden handles to the frieze drawer, thumb-moulded edging to tabletop, on reel-and-bobbin turned legs with plain square stretchers on small bun feet. 2 ft 8 in/81 cm wide. £1500–2000.

George II side table or low '*bois*' with a single drawer in the frieze, small shaped apron and fretted spandrels on four straight chamfered legs. 2 ft 10 in/86 cm wide. £1000–1500.

William and Mary walnut lowboy with quarter-veneered top and cross-banded thumb-moulding with cup and tapered turned legs, serpentine stretchers with central turned finial, on turned bun feet. 2 ft 5 in/74 cm wide. £3500–4000.

George I walnut lowboy with moulded edge to top, projecting drawer mouldings, brass backplates and simple bail handles, with shaped frieze and nicely-shaped tapering cabriole legs with pad feet. 2 ft 6 in/76 cm wide. £4000–6000.

George I walnut lowboy with quarter-veneered top, cross-banded with moulded edge, one single full-length drawer and two small drawers with projecting lip moulding in the frieze, shaped apron and curving cabriole legs with pad feet.
2 ft 4 in/71 cm wide. £3000–4000.

An early 18th-century walnut and featherstrung lowboy, with a crossbanded top and a moulded edge containing three drawers in the arched apron, on cabriole legs with scrolls and pad feet.
£1000–1500.

George I walnut kneehole dressing chest or writing chest, cross-banded with projecting lip moulding to drawers, plain brass backplates to simple bail handles, on neat bracket feet. 2 ft 7 in/79 cm wide. £5000–7000.

A 19th-century English rosewood and brass marquetry kneehole in the style of André-Charles Boulle in premier and contre-partie with a single drawer above a curved apron flanked by two drawers on either side, on outward curving legs. £8000–12 000.

William and Mary burr walnut chest of drawers with decorative feather stringing and narrow cornice below the cross-banded top, the sides also cross-banded, with plinth-moulded base on bun feet. 3 ft 2 in/96.5 cm wide. £4000–6000.

William and Mary flat-fronted chest of drawers in oyster veneer and boxwood stringing with narrow cornice below the cross-banded top, the brass backplates of later date. 3 ft 2 in/96.5 cm wide. £5000–8000.

William and Mary walnut and marquetry flat-fronted chest of drawers with cross-banding and half-round moulding edging the carcase surrounding the drawers, on shaped bracket feet. 3 ft 1 in/94 cm wide. £5000–7000.

Queen Anne walnut chest of drawers with quarter-veneered top, the projecting drawer mouldings cross-banded. A shallow top drawer above three small drawers, a pair and two long graduated drawers with brass backplates and plain bail handles. Carrying-handles on either side. Plinth-moulded base and shaped bracket feet. 3 ft 1 in/94 cm wide. £6000–8000.

Queen Anne walnut bachelors' chest, feather-banded with hinged top supported on pull-out slides flanking two small drawers above three graduated drawers, on plinth-moulded base with plain bracket feet. 2 ft 4 in / 71.5 cm wide. £6000–8000.

George II mahogany chest with moulded edge to top and brushing slide and four graduated drawers, with gilt metal rococo backplates, handles and escutcheons, on plinth-moulded base with plain bracket feet. 3 ft 3 in / 99 cm wide. £2000–3000.

Late 17th-century oak clothes press with fielded panel doors fitted with shelves above, and drawers in the base with plain turned wooden handles, the base with curved bracket feet. 5 ft / 1.52 m wide. £1000–1600.

Queen Anne walnut chest on chest in fine cartouche veneered panels with boxwood and ebony stringing, cross-banded, with lip moulding to the edges and cornice, a cushion drawer below the cornice and the interior fitted with 11 shallow drawers and a secret drawer, on plain bun feet. 3 ft 5 in / 1.04 m wide. £5000–7000.

George I walnut tallboy made in two parts, with cross-banding to the projecting moulding round the drawers and half-round moulding between, with three small drawers at the top and graduated drawers in both halves, on plinth-moulded base with plain bracket feet.
3 ft 5 in/1.04 m wide.
£4000–6000.

Ebonised oak wardrobe from the 'Arts & Crafts' movement of furniture design, after the style of the Glasgow school of C.R. Mackintosh with inlaid oval panels and stringing and a deep drawer in the base, on plain turned bun feet.
£1000–1500.

A 19th-century mahogany linen press or 'housekeeper's cupboard' with plain panelled doors and a secretaire drawer below flanked by two small drawers with three long graduated drawers below, with shaped apron and splayed bracket feet. £2000–3000.

A 19th-century Victorian oak linen press with dentil cornice and arched moulding with leaf-carved surrounds to applied carved mythical beasts and scenes from mythology, and two full-length deep drawers in the base. £1200–1500.

Bow-fronted mahogany chest of drawers cross-banded in satinwood with ebony and boxwood stringing of Sheraton design, with fitted writing drawer above three full-length drawers, on square tapering peg feet with cast brass shoes. 2 ft 10 in/86.5 cm high, 2 ft 11 in/89 cm wide. £3000–4000.

George III satinwood and burr yew wood demilune commode with harewood, stained sycamore and palisander veneer decorating the top wtih four graduated drawers on plain square tapering gaitered feet. £8000–12 000.

George II mahogany serpentine chest with canted corners, with gilt metal rococo handles and escutcheons, on plinth-moulded base with canted bracket feet. 3 ft 8 in / 1.12 m wide. £6000–8000.

George III serpentine-fronted chest in mahogany, the drawer fronts cross-banded to simulate pairs of drawers, with cross-banded canted corners, on plinth-moulded base with canted bracket feet. 3 ft 2 in/96.5 cm wide. £6000–8000.

George III satinwood and partridgewood dressing chest with fitted top drawer and oval veneered panel decorating the top, with slender canted corners on ogee bracket feet. £6000–8000.

George III mahogany serpentine-fronted dressing chest with cockbead surround to three graduated drawers with curved shaped apron on slender splayed feet. £3000–4000.

George III mahogany serpentine-fronted gentleman's commode with rounded corners and gilt brass rococo handles and escutcheons with crisply-carved flowerhead and foliate apron and foliate carving to the curved, scrolled legs and feet. £10 000–15 000.

A 19th-century marquetry and ormolu bombé commode in the French taste with marble top, inlaid with flowers, leaves and ribbons with shaped apron and outward-curving tapering legs with cast gilt metal scroll feet. £2000–3000.

Early 18th-century oak dresser base with plinth-moulded top and three drawers in the frieze, two in the curved, shaped apron, with two-plank potboard below and plain straight legs and feet. £3000–4000.

An 18th-century dresser in oak in North Country style with plank back to shelves and shaped uprights with a central flight of four drawers, flanked by cupboards with drawers above, on shaped bracket feet. £1800–2200.

A 19th-century corner cupboard with dentil moulding and serpentine-shaped base, with glazed doors and plank back, in stained pine with brass hinges and key-plate. £450–650.

Late 18th-century oak dresser base with pierced decorative scrolled apron and three drawers, on plain straight chamfered legs. 5 ft 10 in / 1.77 m wide. £3000–4000.

Late 18th-century full-length oak corner cupboard with plank back and glazed doors above two plain panelled doors in the base. £1000–1500.

George III mahogany secretaire bookcase with centre fall in the breakfronted base with geometric astragal moulding to the glazed doors and fitted with adjustable shelves. 8 ft 11 in/2.72 m high, 4 ft 10 in/1.47 m wide. £8000–12 000.

Regency mahogany secretaire bookcase with applied decorative moulding and brass lattice grilles and pleated silk panels to the cupboards in the base. £6000–8000.

Breakfront library bookcase, late 18th-century, with ebony stringing to the panelled doors and carved mahogany decoration to the glazed doors forming tassels above and below the geometrical glazing bars with grooved stays for adjustable shelves. 9 ft/2.74 m high, 9 ft 9 in/2.97 m wide. £15 000–20 000.

A 19th-century satinwood and marquetry breakfront library bookcase with central broken pediment and arched glazing bars, the doors inlaid and outlined in tulipwood and fitted inside with trays and shelves. 8 ft 9 in / 2.66 m high, 8 ft 4 in/2.54 m wide. £10 000–15 000.

Victorian oak library bookcase in high Gothic style decorated with gargoyles and winged cherubs and fantastic masks with carved scenes of bucolic country life on the base cupboard doors. £1500–2000.

George III mahogany serpentine sideboard, cross-banded in tulipwood with boxwood stringing with single drawer in the centre, flanked by a cellarette drawer and a cupboard, on plain square tapering legs with spade feet. 4 ft 6 in/1.37 m wide. £3000–4000.

George III serpentine sideboard in mahogany and satinwood, inlaid with husks and decorated in the neo-classical taste, with two drawers in the centre flanked by a cellarette drawer and a cupboard, on square tapering legs with spade feet. £4000–6000.

Late 18th-century serpentine sideboard inlaid with small fan spandrels and strung with boxwood with central drawer and cellarette and cupboard on either side, on square tapering legs with spade feet. 5 ft 6 in/1.67 m wide. £3000–4000.

George III mahogany bow-fronted secretaire-sideboard with fitted secretaire drawer in the centre flanked by two deep drawers with cupboards below, with boxwood stringing to the door and drawer fronts and with slender decorative columns and reeded edge to the top. 3 ft 1 in/94 cm high, 5 ft 5 in/1.65 m wide. £2000–3000.

One of a pair of Regency rosewood chiffoniers inlaid with brass, and brass columns supporting the galleried top, and three small drawers above the base with recessed pleated silk panel doors flanked by brass-mounted columns and two drawers inlaid with cut brass. 4 ft 6 in / 1.37 m high, 3 ft 6 in / 1.07 m wide. Pair: £10 000–15 000.

Regency carved rosewood side cabinet or chiffonier with acanthus leaf decoration to the scrolled uprights and pierced brass gallery inlaid with cut brass and with carved and gilded edging to the top and base, with cupboards below flanked by two decorative columns on carved turned feet. £3000–4000.

Regency rosewood and parcel gilt chiffonier with marble top, the sides supported with applied columns in the Egyptian style, with hinged fallfront above two brass lattice grille doors with pleated silk behind. £2000–3000.

Collector's Items

One of the most notable developments in the antique market in recent times has been the growing interest in an enormous range of types of item previously little regarded. A varied selection of these is illustrated in the following pages. Such a wide range of items is included in this category that it is difficult to give meaningful advice in the limited space available here on exactly what may be the coming vogue.

Obviously the usual factors of rarity and condition are very important in this field as in any other. Complete sets and particularly those in their original packaging may, in certain categories, be a great deal more valuable than individual items.

Above all a developing interest in an area of collecting can be pursued economically and finds may be made at every conceivable type of sale and shop. Even if you never acquire any of the rarest antiques a growing collection will be great fun.

An A. W. Taylor's patent treadle sewing machine. £350-400.

Goss Cottages

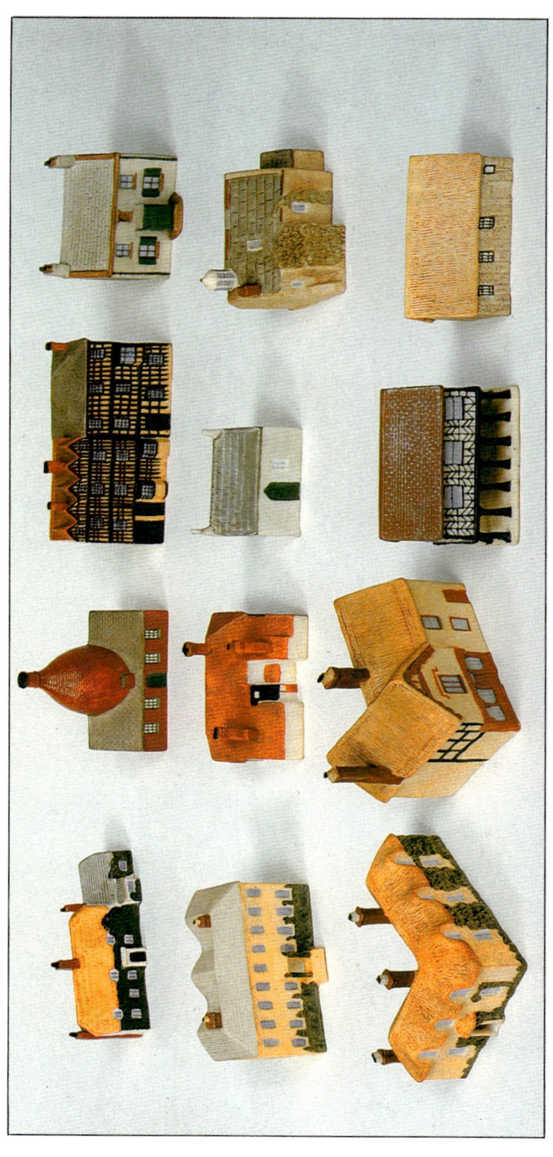

A collection of Goss decorated parian ware cottages. £100-300 for each.

Above A collection of John Gilroy Carlton ware figures. £100-120.

Below A set of Beatles 'Bobb 'n Head' figures. 1964. £130-170.

A Victorian embossed paper lace, hand-coloured letter Valentine. £30-50.

October from an Art Nouveau set of postcards of the months of the year. £150-250 set of 12.

A set of 25 cards of National Costumes by Wills. £2500-3500.

Right Examples from a set of 50 animals and birds in fancy costume by Wills. £800-900 the set.

WILLS'S CIGARETTES

WILLS'S CIGARETTES

WILLS'S CIGARETTES

WILLS'S CIGARETTES

WILLS'S CIGARETTES

WILLS'S CIGARETTES

A selection of teddy bears by Steiff, Bing and Schuco. Left to right: £700-800; £1500-2500; £2800-3200; £900-1000; £2000-2600; £900-1000.

A bisque head doll by Emile Jumean. 17in/43cm. £700-900.

A French bisque head Paris-Bébé doll by Daniel & Cie. 15in/40cm. £1500-2500.

A rare 70mm-scale figure of the Colonel-in-Chief of the Welsh Guards. £800-1200.

Above Right A Britain's U.S. Marine Corps band in the original box. £1800-2300.

Right A Tipp clockwork motorcyclist. *c.* 1950s. 7in/17.5cm. £80-100.

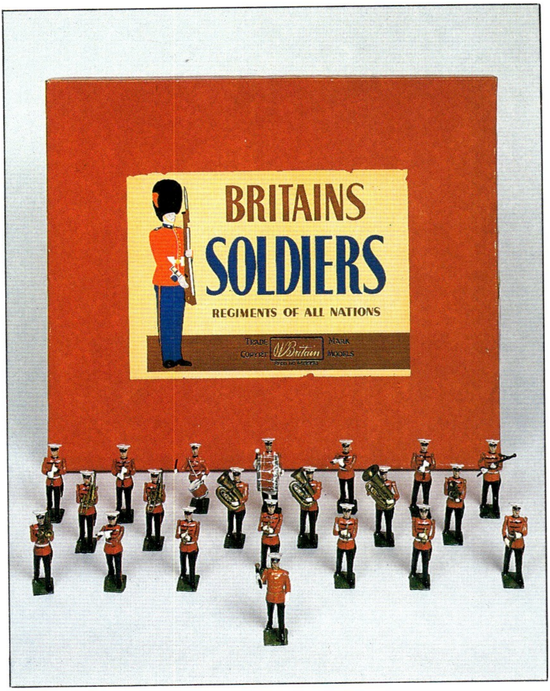

Lead soldiers/clockwork toys

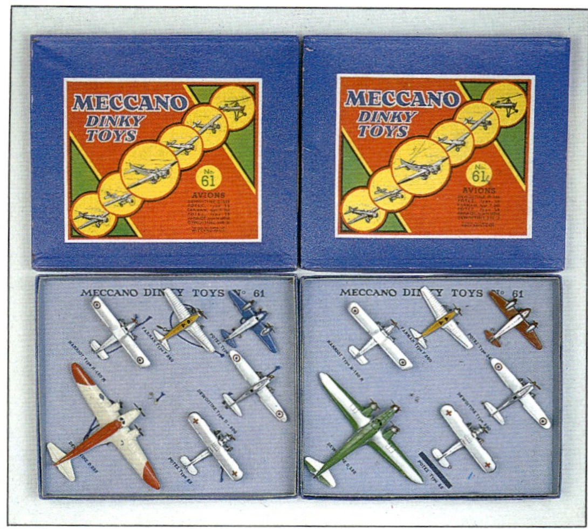

Above Pre World War II aircraft sets by Dinky from a French factory. £1500-2000 each set.

A German tinplate Cadillac by Gama, mid 1950s. £550-650.

Below (Top row) Three Triang clockwork Minic cars. L to R: £200-300; £250-350; £200-250. (Bottom row) Three pre World War II Dinky cars. L to R: £400-500; £300-350; £250-300.

A pot lid depicting the Swedish singer Jenny Lind (*fl.* 1840-1880). £300-500.

Clocks

Few serious clock collectors are totally ignorant about the mechanism and movements of at least one kind of clock. Many people have begun collecting clocks as a result of being given or inheriting a clock of some description which may no longer be in working order. By tinkering about with it they eventually become totally absorbed in the mechanics of clockwork until it becomes a gathering passion. The actual movement of a clock, however, is only one factor which determines the value and rarity of an antique clock. The case-work and the shape and style of dial and hands also help to determine whether a clock is genuine or not.

At first glance, the prices paid for clocks seem to have no rhyme or reason: one clock sells for thousands of pounds while another, to all intents and purpose looking to the uninitiated almost the same, will fetch only a few hundred. It must be appreciated, first and foremost, that every clock of any age has been genuinely repaired in the course of its working life, and much depends on the quality and craftsmanship of those repairs. Many have had their movements altered or completely replaced, others have been codged up at some later date, or put together from bits of another clock of a similar period.

Essential facts

Since the earliest clocks with spring drive and fusee movement are outside the scope of this guide, progress is charted from the beginning of pendulum clocks, first invented in about 1658 and generally credited to John Fromanteel, though there are many other contenders for its origins. Without going into too many technical details, it is essential to know that early pendulum clocks had one hand only, a narrow chapter ring, and were marked with hours and half-hours only. From *c.*1690 the accuracy of the pendulum beat was such that in addition to hours, half-hours and quarters marked on the inside of the chapter ring in Roman numerals, a subsidiary seconds dial was added, marked in Arabic numerals. After this, a minute hand and markings for minutes were added to the outside of the chapter ring, once a longer pendulum replaced the short 'bob pendulum' of early lantern clocks. An intermediate stage, involving a pendulum with a wider swing, produced the 'wing clock'.

Longcase clocks developed in parallel with bracket clocks, both with pendulums but with slightly different movements. The longcase clock allowed for a longer period of going, and early London-made clocks, from *c.*1660, were almost all 8-day going, with two hands and subsidiary seconds dials. 30-hour clocks continued for some time to be made with one hand only, and only quarters marked on chapter rings. 8-day clocks were key-wound, whereas 30-hour clocks were wound by pulling down the endless cord with its various weights and counter-weights.

London and provincial

While London clocks were almost all key-wound 8-day going, provincial clocks were predominantly 30-hour going, which were far cheaper to make. Many provincial makers resorted to a simple deception by giving their clocks dials with winding holes, thus giving the illusion that the clock was an expensive 8-day going clock. Many honest provincial longcase clocks with 30-hour movements were made with one hand only, at least up to *c.*1740. So many, in fact as to indicate a preference rather than a limitation. Large numbers of these simple clocks have been altered at a later date, usually by replacing the 30-hour movement with an 8-day one, with two hands. Often, however, the dial has not been replaced, and a chapter ring with no minute markings quickly betrays this later modification.

The movement of a 30-hour clock was usually of birdcage construction, with upright posts or pillars holding the top and bottom plates together, in essence very similar to the construction of a lantern clock movement. In some cases the posts or pillars were often of fine-quality brass with decorative turning, and many of these have been removed from their provincial cases and converted into 'genuine lantern clocks' particularly during the Victorian period, when spurious signatures of such famous makers as Tompion or Knibb were added.

The movement of an 8-day clock is usually of plate frame construction, where the plates are set at the back and front as opposed to top and bottom, with shorter pillars or posts to hold them together. Where a 30-hour movement has been replaced by an 8-day movement, the shape of the case and dial will help to identify the modification, as well as holes in the plates and the 'seat board' on which the movement rests.

Case work

It will be realized that dial, movement and case must be in accord if the clock is authentic. Brass dials may have been substituted for later plain white dials – in some cases, arched dials have been put into a clock and the whole hood and case has been altered to accommodate them. As a general rule, cases follow the same periods and styles as those of furniture, certainly for London-made clocks, and a time-lag of as much as 20 years may occur between fashionable designs in London and the provinces. Early London longcase clocks were ebonised, either with ebony veneer on an oak carcase, or with stained pear wood, or in ebonised oak. It seems that early veneers and marquetry were laid on oak carcases for a longer period than furniture, which was generally made with a pine carcase from the late 17th century onwards.

Provincial longcase clocks were not made in any quantity much before *c.*1730, and were either in plain oak or in mahogany veneer, since the timber was shipped into Liverpool and was readily available. Although their styles may lag behind London clocks, provincial clocks were seldom of the plain, small, architectural designs of early London clocks. Their designs more or less coincide with the change from square-faced dials to arched dials.

On London longcase clocks, the arch of the dial was often simply decorative, or displayed the name of the maker, or was used for the strike/silent dial. In the provinces the arch was often filled with a lunar dial, and in London, Liverpool and other port towns there might be a tidal dial for high and low water, but these are more rare than moon phase dials. Automata were very fashionable from about *c.*1720 and the same rocking mechanism which drove the lunar dial was employed to drive all manner of little clockwork scenes.

Bracket clocks and carriage clocks

The development of bracket clocks follows slightly different lines in terms of movement, though the design of cases runs parallel to those of longcase clocks. The driving power was supplied by a spring enclosed in a drum. When the drum was turned with a key, a gut or chain was wound round a metal cone with a spiral track known as the fusee, which regulated the speed of the drive. Instead of a striking mechanism, many bracket clocks had a 'pull repeat' which, when a cord was pulled, repeated the stroke of the last quarter or half hour, depending on the mechanism. Backplates of bracket clocks are visible through the glass panels of the case, and were beautifully engraved with flowers, leaves, and often a cartouche enclosing the maker's name. From about 1720 onwards, the size of bracket clocks increased and many were made with anchor escapements instead of the original verge so far used in association with the fusee.

The miniaturized version of the bracket clock, the carriage clock, was originally the sole province of French clockmakers who equipped these little clocks – the mignonette was only about 4½in/11.4cm high – with chimes known as the 'petite sonnerie' or 'grande sonnerie', often combined with minute repeaters and even alarm mechanisms. A simpler version of this complicated and expensive mechanism was first produced by French maker Paul Garnier in the first half of the 19th century and this cheaper version of the 'pendule de voyage' proved extremely popular in England, where many of them were made by well-known London makers.

Regulators, skeletons and Acts of Parliament

Until 1752, time in England was reckoned by 'sundial' time, regulated to a certain extent by leap years. Sidereal time, equal to 365 days 6 hours 9 minutes, was adopted in 1752, and the regulating of time became an important factor to clockmakers, although it still varied by a matter of minutes from east to west, north to south. The simplest, most accurate of mechanisms were devised, called 'regulator clocks' which were essentially functional and stripped of all decoration. Early regulator clocks, with mercury-filled pendulums and mirrored back-boards, are extremely attractive though later ones tend to be more functional and less pleasing. They might be said to be the forerunners of the skeleton clock, though the design of these is usually attributed to French clockmakers. Skeleton clocks first appeared in England in the mid-19th century, and many of them are of wonderfully Gothic design. Out of fashion for many years, they are now a growing collectors' market.

One curious oddity is the naming of wall-mounted tavern

clocks 'Act of Parliament' clocks. Such clocks were well-known long before a tax on clocks and watches was imposed in 1797, when the populace is supposed to have hidden their own clocks and watches to avoid paying tax and relied instead on large wall-mounted clocks in taverns and other public places. Certainly the Act had nothing to do with the 'Definition of Time' Act which came into force in 1880 when Greenwich mean time was accepted by all regions with the exception of Ireland which maintained Dublin time until 1917.

Notable clockmakers

London

Bradley, Langley. Clockmakers' company member from 1695–1738. Longcase and bracket, turret clocks.

East, Edward. Born 1602. Died 1696. Famous for clocks and watches. Chief Clockmaker to the King 1660.

Ebsworth, John. Clockmakers' company freeman 1665–99. Lantern, longcase, bracket clocks and watches.

Fromanteel, Ahasuerus 1. Born 1607. Died 1693. Introduced the pendulum to Britain 1658. Most important clockmaker of all.

Fromanteel, Ahasuerus and John. Sons of above. Transferred to Amsterdam *c.*1680.

Gould, Christopher. Died 1718. Famous for longcase, bracket clocks and watches.

Knibb, John and Joseph. Sons of Samuel Knibb. A famous name in lantern clocks and longcase clocks.

Loomes, Thomas. London clockmaker from 1649–65. Mainly known for lantern clocks.

Quare, Daniel. Born 1649. Died 1724. Famous clockmaker, known for longcase, bracket clocks and watches.

Tompion, Thomas. Born 1639. Died 1713. Best known if not most famous English clockmaker, known for lantern and longcase clocks, but principally made watches.

Windmills, Joseph. Worked in London from 1671–*c.*1723, known for lantern and longcase clocks.

Provincial

Bellman, William. Lancashire. Working 1790–*c.*1812.
Benson, Whitehaven. Working from *c.*1750–98.
Clifton, John. Liverpool. Working from 1777–94.
Crofts, Thomas. Leeds. Working 1752–56.
Finney, John, Joseph I and Joseph II. Liverpool. *c.*1761–90
Halifax, George. Halifax. 1725–1811.
Halifax, John, Joseph and Thomas. Barnsley. 1695–1789.
Lister, Thomas. Halifax. 1745–1814.
Lomax, James. Blackburn. 1749–1814.
Moore, Thomas. Ipswich. *c.*1740–*c.*1756.
Nicholson, William. Whitehaven. *c.* 1735–65.
Nickols, Isaac. Wells. ? London *c.*1700–40.
Rollison, Dollif. Father and son. Halton, Leeds. *c.*1720–*c.*1790.
Rowntree, Ralph. York. 1673–? (married 1696).
Rowntree, Robert. York. Working 1822–34.
Standring, Bolton. 1712–82.
Williamson, John. Leeds *c.*1683–1748.
Wilson, John. Peterborough. 1757–95.

Late 17th-century brass lantern clock by Thomas Dyde, London. Circular dial with engraved face, chapter ring with subsidiary seconds ring, central calendar ring, posted frame with urn finials, pierced and engraved dolphin cresting pieces. 13⅜in/34cm high. £1800–2500.

Late 17th-century brass lantern clock with circular dial and face engraved with tulips and leaves, subsidiary seconds ring, posted frame with urn finials, outside countwheel with pendulum swinging between two trains. 14½in/37cm high. £2000–2800.

A 17th-century wing lantern clock with single steel hand and engraved face, chapter ring with subsidiary seconds ring, pierced and engraved dolphin cresting pieces, posted frame with urn finials, countwheel strike. 16in/41cm high. £2200–3000.

Small-sized brass lantern clock *c.*1720 by John Parkes & William King, London, made for the Turkish market with decorative foliate spandrels, Islamic numerals, posted frame with urn finials. 9in/23cm high. £700–1000.

A 17th-century lantern clock by Thomas Wheeler *c.*1700 with narrow chapter ring, subsidiary seconds ring, single hand, engraved face, dolphin cresting pieces, posted frame with urn finials. 15¾in/40cm high. £1400–1600.

A 17th-century brass lantern clock by John Pennock with narrow silvered chapter ring, single steel hand and subsidiary seconds ring, posted frame with urn finials. 15in/38cm high. £2000–2800.

Early 18th-century brass lantern clock by Step Harris, Tonbridge. Wide chapter ring of 'sheep's head' provincial proportions, subsidiary seconds ring, outside countwheel strike. 15in/38cm high. £1200–1500.

A 19th-century lantern alarum clock with 30-hour movement by William Flint, Ashford. Posted frame, arched silvered dial with engraved decorative spandrels, central alarum dial, single hand and bell strike. 8¼in/21cm high. £900–1200.

Late 17th-century walnut wall clock with dolphin cresting piece in the arch, square dial, sliding hood, narrow chapter ring and cherubs' head spandrels, 30-hour movement with a quarter chime on 8 bells. *c.*1669–1718. Anchor escapement. 25⅛ in / 64 cm high. £3000–5000.

'Act of Parliament' timepiece by J. Ireland, London. White-painted wooden dial, pendulum enclosed by black lacquer and chinoiserie case, outside subsidiary seconds ring with arabic numerals, mid-18th-century, with 18 in / 46 cm diameter dial. £2800–4000.

Above Wall clock *c.*1740 with 9 in / 23 cm diameter brass dial, with alarum ring and alarum train striking hours on a single bell. Anchor escapement. £1200–1800.

Early 19th-century ebonised wall bracket clock by Thwaites & Reed with applied brass mouldings, decorative pierced spandrels and arch decoration with fusee movement, mounted on wall bracket, with carrying-handle, *c.*1820. Anchor escapement. 16⅛ in / 41 cm high, 2 ft 2 in / 66 cm overall. £750–1100.

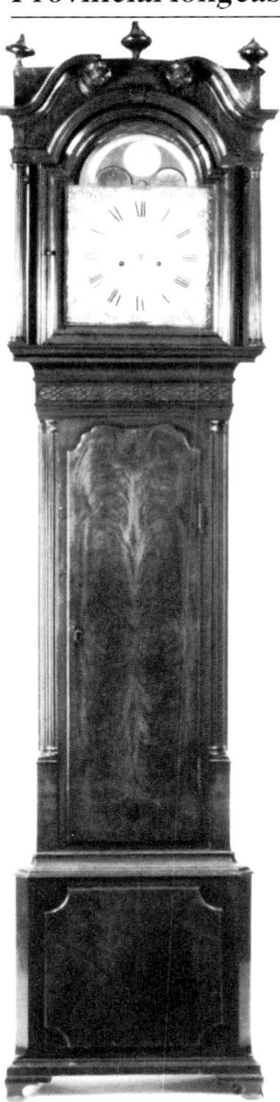

George II mahogany longcase clock by Whitehurst, Derby, with square-topped hood with three turned finials and applied carved horned pediment. Arched dial with quadri-circular calendar aperture and moon phase indicator in the lunette. 8-day movement with anchor escapement, striking on a single bell. *c.*1740. 7½ ft / 2.30 m high. £2500–3200.

An 18th-century red lacquer and chinoiserie longcase clock by George Washbourne, Gloucester with simplified 'pagoda-topped' hood with brass finials. 12 in/30 cm arched brass dial, subsidiary seconds and date rings, twin train 8-day five pillar movement with anchor escapement and inside countwheel strike. 7 ft 9½ in / 2.38 m high. £2100–2800.

George II cream and apple-green lacquer longcase clock by Isaac Nickals, Wells, Norfolk *c.* 1740 with arch topped hood with whale's tail cresting. 19 in/48 cm arched brass dial, silvered chapter ring with subsidiary seconds ring, calendar aperture and centre sweep seconds hand. £4000–5000.

Detail of dial. Moon phase and high water indicator in the lunette with strike/silent lever in the arch. Four subsidiary dials indicating days of the week, month, repeat/not repeat, and strike quarters/not-strike quarters.

Right The three train 8-day five pillar movement with anchor escapement and quarters striking on three bells.

Early George III green lacquered longcase clock by Benjamin Smith, Canterbury with moulded broken-arched pediment with decorative finials, the case decorated overall in red and gold lattice. 16in/41cm arched brass dial with subsidiary seconds ring, calendar aperture and strike/silent dial. Five pillar movement with rack strike and anchor escapement. *c.*1770. 7ft 4½in/2.25m high. £2500–3500.

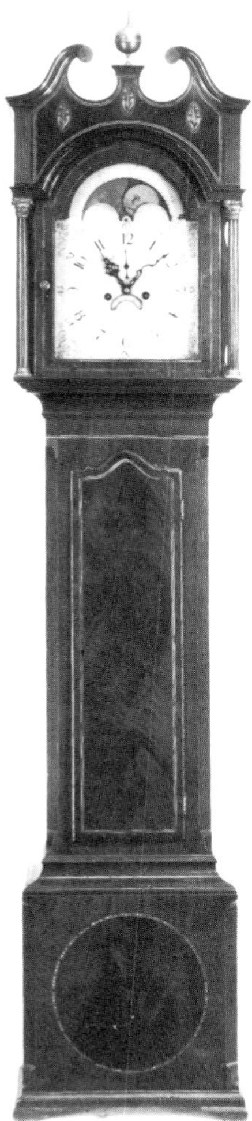

Georgian mahogany longcase clock by George Taylor, Sherborne with arched hood and horned pediment. 12 in/30 cm white-painted dial with subsidiary seconds ring, calendar aperture, moon phase indicator, twin train 8-day movement with anchor escapement. 7 ft 8 in/2.35 m high. £1200–2000.

Georgian mahogany longcase clock by Thomas Harrison, Liverpool, with moulded horned pediment. 18 in/46 cm arched brass dial with silvered chapter ring and subsidiary seconds ring, engraved face, moon phase indicator in the arch. Twin train 8-day movement with anchor escapement. 7 ft 8 in/2.35 m high. £800–1100.

George III mahogany longcase clock by Samuel Collier, Eccles, *c.*1770 with elaborate hood with decorative finials and gilded horned pediment. White enamel dial with face decorated with pastoral scene, subsidiary seconds ring and calendar aperture, with moon phase indicator in the arch. Twin train 8-day movement with anchor escapement. 7 ft 10 in / 2.40 m high. £800–1100.

George III mahogany longcase clock by John May, Southampton with arch topped hood and decorative finials. 12 in / 30 cm arched brass dial, silvered chapter ring and face, subsidiary seconds ring, calendar aperture and strike/silent dial. Twin train 8-day movement with anchor escapement. *c.*1773. 8 ft / 2.44 m high. £2000–2500.

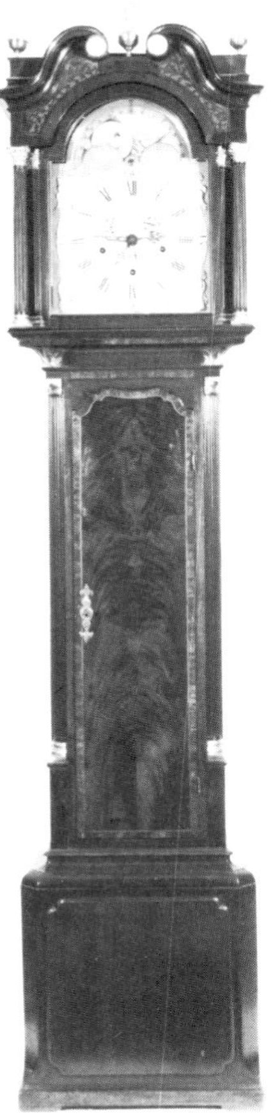

Georgian mahogany longcase clock by Thomas Finney, Liverpool, with horned pediment and decorative finials. 12 in/30 cm arched brass dial, silvered chapter ring, sweep centre seconds hand and calendar hand, strike/silent lever in the centre and tune indicator changing each day. Three train movement with anchor escapement and 12 bells playing music, and moon phase indicator in arch. 7 ft 7 in/2.32 m high. £3000–4000.

George III mahogany longcase clock by William Newton, Lawson-le-Willows with modified 'pagoda-topped' hood with arched dial and rococo spandrels. 18 in/46 cm diameter brass dial with silvered chapter ring, three winding squares, subsidiary seconds ring and lunette with moon phases. Musical three train movement striking on eight graduated bells. 9 ft 10 in/*c.*3.0 m high. £2000–3000.

Left William and Mary marquetry longcase clock by Edward Burgis, London, with square-topped hood with simple moulding and glazed bull's eye in waist panel door. 10½in/27cm square brass dial and cherub spandrels with silvered chapter ring, subsidiary seconds ring, calendar aperture and strike/silent dial. Twin train month going movement with six pillars and outside countwheel strike. *c.*1690. 6ft 9⅞in/2.08m high. £7000–8000.

Centre William and Mary marquetry longcase clock by Francis Clement, London with single steel hand and alarum with glazed bull's eye in waist panel door. 10in/25cm square brass dial with calendar ring in the centre. Twin train 8-day movement with six pillars, anchor escapement and outside countwheel strike. *c.* 1677–99. £4000–6000.

Right Early 18th-century walnut veneered and seaweed marquetry longcase clock by Thomas Taylor, Holborn, with square-topped hood with simple moulding and twist-turned columns, with glazed bull's eye in waist panel door. 10½in/27cm square brass dial with cherub's head spandrels, silvered chapter ring, subsidiary seconds ring and calendar aperture. Twin train 8-day five pillar movement with anchor escapement and outside countwheel strike. 6ft 9in/2.05m high. £4000–5000.

Left Early 18th-century red lacquer longcase clock with moulded ogee cushion pediment and glazed bull's eye in waist panel door. 16 in / 41 cm square brass dial with subsidiary seconds ring, calendar aperture, alarum train and harboured winding holes. Twin train movement with turned ring pillars and anchor escapement. 6 ft 9 in/2.05 m high. £4000–6000.

Centre Early 18th-century walnut veneered and marquetry longcase clock with carved pediment and applied cresting piece and twist-turned columns, glazed bull's eye in waist panel door. 10¾ in / 27.5 cm square brass dial with silvered chapter ring, subsidiary seconds ring and calendar aperture, with matted finish to centre of brass face. Twin train 8-day movement with five pillars, anchor escapement and inside countwheel strike. 7 ft 4 in / 2.24 m high. £7000–9000.

Right An 18th-century walnut veneered and seaweed marquetry longcase by William Sellers, Long Acre with square-topped hood and glazed bull's eye in waist panel door. 12 in / 30 cm square brass dial, crown and putti spandrels, silvered chapter ring, subsidiary seconds ring, calendar aperture. Twin train five pillar movement, month-going with bolt and shutter maintaining power, anchor escapement and outside countwheel strike. 7 ft 1 in/2.16 m high. £6000–8000.

An 18th-century walnut veneered longcase clock by Obadiah Gardner, London with square-topped hood. 16 in/41 cm arched brass dial with silvered chapter ring, subsidiary seconds ring, calendar aperture and rise and fall regulation lever within arch. Twin train 8-day movement with anchor escapement. *c.* 1712–27. 6 ft 11 in/2.11 m high. £2800–3500.

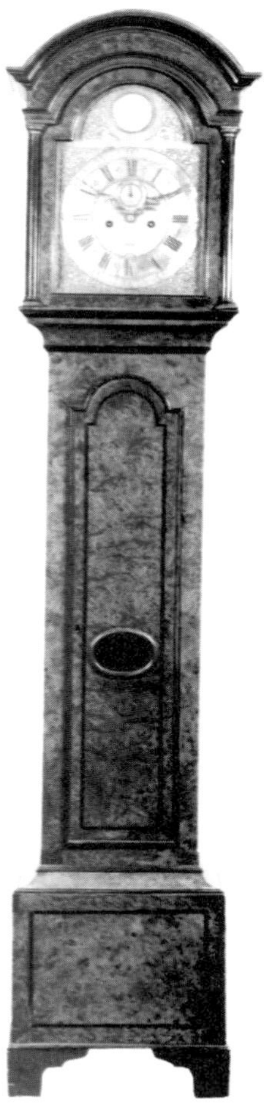

Queen Anne burr elm longcase clock with arch-topped hood and glazed bull's eye in waist panel door. 18 in/46 cm arched brass dial with mask and foliate spandrels, silvered chapter ring, subsidiary seconds ring, and calendar aperture. 8-day movement with anchor escapement. 7 ft 2½ in/2.2 m high. £2000–3000.

Georgian mahogany longcase clock with ogee pediment and arch-topped hood. 12 in/30 cm arched brass dial with strike/silent indicator in arch. Silvered chapter ring and subsidiary seconds ring and calendar aperture. Twin train 8-day movement with anchor escapement. £3000–4000.

George II longcase clock in mahogany with arch-topped hood and decorative finials by Bennett, Greenwich. White enamelled dial with gold-painted decoration with subsidiary seconds ring. Twin train 8-day movement with anchor escapement. 7 ft 6 in/2.3 m high. £1200–1800.

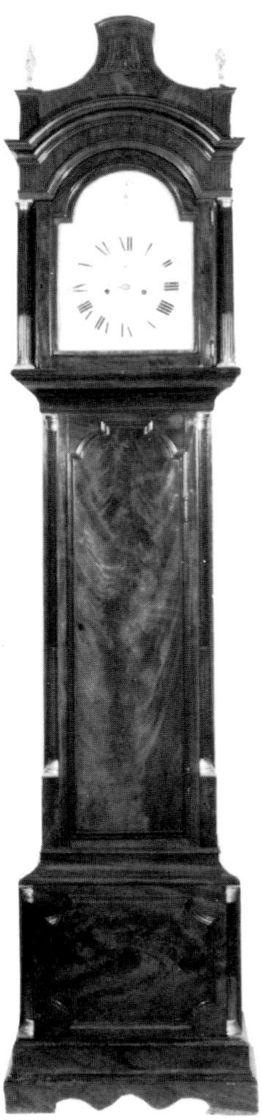

Georgian mahogany longcase clock by Samuel Toulmin, London with ogee pediment and decorative finials. Arched Bilston enamel dial signed Samuel Toulmin, Strand, London. Subsidiary seconds ring and strike/silent lever in arch. Twin train 8-day movement with anchor escapement. 8 ft 6 in/2.6 m high. £3000–4000.

George III mahogany longcase clock by James McCabe, Royal Exchange, London *c.* 1781 with arch-topped case and circular 11 in/28 cm white-painted dial with numeral sweep. An 8-day movement with anchor escapement and single strike bell. 6½ ft/2 m high. £3000–4000.

Late Victorian rosewood and ivory inlaid longcase clock with arch-topped hood and decorative pediment. 19 in / 48 cm repoussé brass dial with lacquered brass indicators and applied silver numerals. Month-going three train movement with musical chime striking on eight cylindrical gongs. £1200–1800.

Detail of dial.

Late 17th-century ebonised striking alarum clock by George Etherington, London *c.*1684 with oblong side-glasses and cushion-topped case with carrying-handle and small decorative finials. 7 in / 18 cm square brass dial with matted centre, silvered chapter ring, calendar aperture and false pendulum aperture, and alarum disc in the centre. Subsidiary dials for strike / silent regulation, pendulum locking, day of the week indicator, rise and fall pendulum adjustment. Twin train five pillar fusee movement with verge escapement and pull quarter repeat on three bells with alarum train. 16⅞ in / 43 cm high. £4000–5000.

Late 17th-century basket-topped bracket clock by Langley Bradley, London, with square brass dial and cherub spandrels, with the basket-top chased with scrolls and cherubs. Silvered chapter ring, calendar aperture, fusee movement with pull quarter repeat. 13¾ in / 35 cm high. £2000–3000.

Early 18th-century bracket timepiece with gilt metal mounts to the cushion-topped case and S-scroll carrying handle, with oblong side glasses. 6 in / 15 cm square brass dial with cherub spandrels, silvered chapter ring and pendulum aperture, pull quarter repeat and verge escapement. 15¾ in / 40 cm high. £1500–2000.

George III ebonised bracket clock by Jasper Taylor, Holborn, with moulded cushion-topped case and brass carrying handle, chased spandrels, calendar and pendulum apertures and strike / silent indicator in arch. Fusee movement with verge escapement and pull quarter repeat with chimes on six bells. 17¾in / 45 cm high. £1500–2000.

George III lacquer bracket clock by Jos. Herring, London *c.*1767 with cushion-topped case and brass carrying handle. Chased spandrels, calendar aperture and pendulum aperture with fusee movement and verge escapement. 17¾in / 45 cm high. £2000–2500.

Ebonised bracket clock by Edward East, London *c.*1735 with cushion-topped case with carrying handle and flame and urn finials. Arched brass dial with chased spandrels, calendar aperture and pendulum aperture with strike/silent indicator in arch. Fusee movement with verge escapement and added quarter strike on six bells. 17¾in / 45 cm high. £1500–2500.

Ebony veneered bracket clock by Francis Gregg, Covent Garden with moulded bell-topped case and gilt brass carrying handle. 7 in/18 cm arched brass dial with silvered chapter ring, calendar aperture and subsidiary dials for pendulum adjustment and strike no quarters/no hours/strike all. Three train movement with latched plates and dial, chiming quarters on six bells. (Later anchor escapement). 18⅞ in/48 cm high. £3000–4000.

Late Georgian scarlet lacquer bracket clock by Frederick Miller, Chelsea, with pagoda-topped case and fretted brass side pieces. 7 in/18 cm silvered dial with engraved decoration and strike/silent indicator in arch. Twin train movement with anchor escapement. 20 in/51 cm high. £4500–5500.

Georgian ebony and gilt metal mounted quarter-chiming bracket clock by Richard Grove, London with pagoda-style top and pineapple finials with side carrying handles and ornate gilt metal mounts. Arched brass dial with strike/silent indicator in arch, crown aperture and calendar aperture and matted finish to centre. Three train movement with verge escapement, striking quarters on eight bells. 2 ft 1¼ in/64 cm high. £4000–5000.

Regency musical bracket clock in ebony and ormulu with urn finials and central pineapple finial by Spencer & Perkins, London. White enamel dial and subsidiary dials for calendar and tune selection, three train fusee movement with verge escapement striking tunes on ten bells, with pull repeat. 2 ft 3⅛ in / 69 cm high. £2000–2500.

Regency mahogany bracket clock with pagoda-top, by James McCabe, London with cut brass inlaid decoration, silvered face with strike/silent indicator and pendulum adjustment dial. Three train fusee movement with anchor escapement, chiming quarters on eight bells. 2 ft 7 in / 79 cm high. £3500–4200.

George III provincial mahogany bracket clock by John Curle, Kelso with moulded caddy-topped case, arched brass dial with painted lunette with moon phase indicator. Three train fusee movement with anchor escapement. £1100–1800.

George III mahogany bracket clock by Dwerrihouse & Carter, London with arch-topped case and carrying handle *c.*1808–15. Strike/silent subsidiary dial and pendulum adjustment dial in arch, with fusee movement and anchor escapement with pull repeat. 15⅜ in / 39 cm high. £1200–1800.

Small-sized ebonised bracket clock by Johnson, London with arch-topped case and carrying handle, chased spandrels, silvered chapter ring and subsidiary dials for chime/silent and slow/fast in arch. Three train fusee movement with anchor escapement chiming quarters on eight bells. 14⅜ in / 36.5 cm high. £800–1200.

Regency mahogany bracket clock by John Sheldrake, Norwich with lion's mask side handles and moulded gadroon-topped case with carrying handle. Fusee movement and anchor escapement. 17¾ in / 45 cm high. £500–900.

Regency mahogany timepiece with ebony stringing and side carrying handles with lancet-shaped case and circular white enamel dial. Fusee movement and anchor escapement. 13 in / 33 cm high. £450–650.

Small-sized Regency mahogany bracket clock by James McCabe, Royal Exchange *c.* 1781 with architectural pediment, arched side glass and engine-turned dial. Fusee movement and later lever escapement. 9¼ in / 23.5 cm high. £350–700.

A 19th-century walnut bracket clock by French, Royal Exchange, with elaborately-carved case with Prince of Wales' Feathers, ears of corn and leaves. Engraved silvered dial, three train fusee movement and quarter strike on eight bells. £300–500.

A 19th-century rosewood clock by Viner, London with circular white enamel dial, fusee movement, anchor escapement and pull repeat. 13 in/33 cm high. £300–600.

Ebonised miniature bracket clock by Dwerrihouse & Carter, London with arched silvered face and carrying handle to case. Fretted side panels, strike/silent dial below the dial, fusee movement and anchor escapement *c.* 1780–1815. 7⅞ in/20 cm high. £800–1200.

Late 19th-century chiming bracket clock in 18th-century taste with pagoda-topped case with decorative flame finials, ormolu mounts and side handles. Pierced brass side panels, arched brass dial with chime/silent and Cambridge/Westminster subsidiary dials. Three train movement and anchor escapement. 28⅜ in/72 cm high. £1200–1800.

Left Regency mahogany regulator timepiece by James McCabe, Royal Exchange, London. 12in/30cm circular dial and subsidiary dials for hours and seconds. Centre sweep minute hand, six pillar movement with maintaining power and dead-beat escapement. Pendulum suspended from 'A' bracket mounted on seat board with screw adjustment. *c.*1781. 6ft 8¼in/2.04m high. £5000–7000.

Centre A 19th-century regulator timepiece by Tydeman, Stowmarket with 12in/30cm silvered dial, sweep centre minute hand and subsidiary dials for hours and seconds. 8-day movement with dead-beat escapement and maintaining power, glazed mercurial pendulum with beat pendulum adjustment and mirrored backboard. 6ft 1½in/1.87m high. £2500–4000.

Right Victorian ebonised regulator timepiece with dead-beat escapement and maintaining power. Silvered skeleton chapter ring and subsidiary dials for seconds and hours, with glazed mercurial pendulum. 6ft 4in/1.93m high. £3000–4000.

Carriage timepiece in heavy cast brass case by Barwise, London with central carrying handle with lion's mask sockets and anthemion and acanthus-leaf decoration *c.*1790. Engine-turned silver dial with fusee movement and lever escapement. 5⅞in/15cm high. £1500–2000.

Fine mid-19th-century English engraved gilt-brass carriage clock by James McCabe, London with Corinthian column supports. Twin train chain fusee movement, typical lever escapement, striking and repeating hours on gong. Silvered dial and blue steel hands. *c.* 1781. £4000–5000.

Plain brass carriage clock with engine-turned face surround by E. White, London. White enamel dial with subsidiary seconds dial, twin train chain fusee movement and lever escapement. 8½in/21.5cm high. £3000–4000.

Decorative carriage timepiece by Finnegans, London, in silver and tortoiseshell case inlaid with floral decoration with carrying handle on small ball feet. 4½in/11.5cm high. £300–400.

French carriage clock in 'corniche' case with lever movement and five-minute repeat. 5¼in/13.5cm high. £350–500.

French carriage clock with elaborately decorated surround to dial, with five minute repeat and push repeat and lever movement. 5⅞in/15cm high. £200–450.

Miniature brass carriage clock or 'mignonette' with white enamel dial and subsidiary date dial, lever movement and push repeat. 2⅞in/7.2cm high. £350–500.

Carved ebonised carriage clock by Charles Frodsham, London with silvered dial within an engraved foliate brass surround with fusee movement and lever escapement. £1200–1800.

Mahogany mantel clock of waisted balloon shape by Metcalf, London *c.*1781–1825. White enamel dial with subsidiary seconds ring, fusee movement and anchor escapement. 18¾in/47.5cm high. £1500–2000.

Early Regency balloon clock by Johnson, Grey's Inn Passage, London in mahogany with moulded ogee pediment and pineapple finial and dummy side carrying handles. Fusee movement and anchor escapement. 17¾in/45cm high. £1000–1500.

Late 18th-century early balloon-shaped timepiece by Weeks, Coventry Street, *c.*1790 with brass drum case and white enamel dial on painted decorative base with pierced brass skirt and curving scroll feet. 15⅜in/39cm high. £800–1200.

A 19th-century brass skeleton timepiece with single train movement, narrow silvered chapter ring, platform and lever escapement. 12½in/32cm high. £550–750.

Right A 19th-century skeleton clock of steeple design with scalloped silvered chapter ring surmounted by strike/silent indicator on turned brass posts. Three train movement chiming on eight bells and a gong. £1500–1800.

Fine brass skeleton timepiece of Gothic design by Vaughan, Bristol, on marble plinth. Fusee movement and anchor escapement. 15in/38cm high. £700–900.

A 19th-century rosewood four-glass mantel clock by Dent, London, with silvered face and engraved spandrels. Fusee movement with anchor escapement, strike / silent bar and pull repeat. 11⅜ in / 29 cm high. £850–1250.

A 19th-century French mantel clock veneered in red tortoiseshell with ormolu mounts, enamelled numerals inset in decorative brass dial with subsidiary seconds panels with arabic numerals. 18½ in / 47 cm high. £550–700.

Victorian Boulle mantel clock veneered in tortoiseshell and cut brass with enamel numerals to the decorative brass face, with heavy ormolu mounts in rococo style. 18½ in / 47 cm high. £450–700.

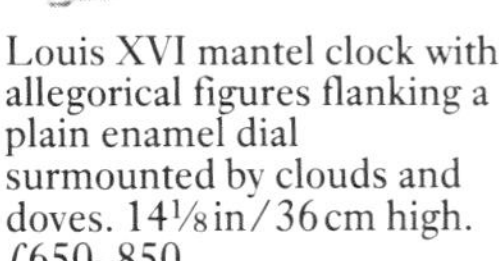

Louis XVI mantel clock with allegorical figures flanking a plain enamel dial surmounted by clouds and doves. 14⅛ in/36 cm high. £650–850.

Silver-gilt and tortoiseshell mantel timepiece with enamel surrounds, decorated in 'Watteau' idyllic pastoral scenes with putti surmounting the side pillars, mounted on four seated lions. 5¾ in/14.5 cm high. £500–700.

Ormolu mantel timepiece in the shape of a classical urn by Grant, Fleet Street with white enamel dial, fusee movement and anchor escapement. 10¼ in/26 cm high. £1000–1500.

A German brass mantel clock, the circular copper face with black enamelled numerals and hands mounted in a brass case of flattened circular form on brass supports with bevelled glass panels on a rectangular base. 15½in/39cm high. £200–250.

A stylish 'Egyptianesque' figural timepiece, the circular face with roman numerals flanked by outspread wings in gilt and blue patination, mounted on a massive block of green onyx before which an Egyptianesque girl in gilt, blue and brown patinated/bronze adopts a stylish pose, the whole raised on a brown variegated rectangular marble base. 20in/51cm high. £1800–2300.

A Liberty & Co. 'English Pewter' timepiece, designed by Archibald Knox, the upright rectangular case having circular face with copper-coloured numerals with red-enamelled 'berry' forms against shaded blue and green enamelling, flanked by stylised entrelacs, leaves and berries. 8in/20.5cm high. £1200–1600.

Silver

Techniques and tools

The techniques and tools of the silversmith have changed remarkably little down the centuries, and craftsmen who make silver by hand today use much the same methods as silversmiths did generations ago. Until the end of the 17th century, English silver was largely made from sheet metal, laboriously beaten out from ingots and then hammered and shaped. The hollow part of a bowl, jug, dish or pot was made in one piece from sheet silver which was hammered out in a 'sinking block' until the shape of a shallow bowl was achieved, and then over a 'raising stake', until the shallow bowl was transformed into the body of a vessel.

An alternative method used from the late 17th century for making hollow ware was to shape a piece of sheet metal into a cone or cylinder, seam it together with solder and then hammer it into shape. This method was used for straight-sided tankards, mugs and coffee pots and the seam can sometimes be detected as a faint hairline, usually following the line of the handle. Vessels made in this way were finished with a sprung wire round the rim. All the additional parts – foot rim, handle, girdle, spout or decoration – were 'applied' or soldered on to the body.

Any parts not soldered but detachable had to be assayed and marked. Thus the lids of covered tankards and cups have a separate set of marks, as do lids of coffee pots and teapots. Some heavy-cast decorative borders of salvers and tazza were not soldered but simply joined, and heavy cast handles of soup tureens are usually bolted to the lids. Any finials which unscrew and any stands which are detachable or made as a separate entity, and sometimes even cast feet must all have the 'sterling' mark of the lion passant at least, if not a complete set of marks. Obviously, all the marks on the various parts of a single piece must be of the same period if it is genuine and authentic.

English silver plate

Gold and silver have been collectively known as 'plate' since Elizabethan days. The name is derived from the Spanish 'plata' which actually means silver. In its pure form, silver, like gold, is too soft to endure, and has always been alloyed with small quantities of harder metal, usually copper with which it has an affinity. In England, the standard proportion of pure silver which constitutes 'sterling' silver is 92.5 per cent pure silver and was first laid down in 1300 by King Edward I. Apart from a brief period from 1697–1720 this standard has remained unchanged to this day. Gold and silver are weighed in Troy weight, slightly different from avoirdupois or metric, and includes the archaic 'dwt' or pennyweight. One Troy ounce is equal to 20 dwt and represents 0.9115 of one ounce avoirdupois.

These weights and measures are important to the potential buyer of antique silver – or indeed any sterling silver – because when the weight of an object is quoted it represents the silver alloy and not the pure silver alone, which will be 7.5 per cent less than the total weight. This is also a point to remember when comparing the price of antique silver with the bullion price quoted on financial pages which is of course for pure silver.

From the earliest times until towards the end of the 19th century, silver was extracted from its ore by a process known as 'leaching' which removed all impurities except for any gold there might be. After 1884 silver was extracted by an electrolytic process and contains no trace of any other elements at all. Almost all antique silver contains minute traces of gold, and it may be this factor which gives old silver a bloom and depth of shine which is not found in silver extracted by modern methods.

Styles and periods

Early English silver (up to *c.* 1700)

The massive style of Continental silver seems to have had little influence on English silversmiths, at least until the end of the 17th century. Designs were simple and decoration showed the Dutch influence which came to England with the return of Charles II from The Hague in 1660, and then with William of Orange in 1688. Decorative motifs were mostly of flowers and leaves, embossed, chased or punched into the sheet metal, and little cast decoration was applied or added. Cut-card work was used to great effect by English silversmiths from the latter years of the 17th and early 18th centuries. A sheet of silver was cut or pierced in a decorative design and then soldered round the body or rim of a vessel, sometimes as a decorative border, often in the shape of a calyx or as leaves cupping the base.

From the 1680s onwards there was a fashion for 'chinoiserie' and oriental designs were often engraved on grander silverware. Armorials and cartouches were also engraved on silver belonging to the nobility and the gentry. In 1685, threats of religious persecution brought many Huguenot silversmiths to England who brought with them techniques which had not been used by English silversmiths before, as well as introducing the grander, heavier shapes and designs of Continental silverware.

Queen Anne (*c.*1700–30)

The great period of Queen Anne silver was the result of a marriage between the simple lines of English silver and the casting and working techniques brought over by the Huguenots. At this period too, the social fabric of England was changing and there was a great demand for silver of all kinds. The custom of tea and coffee drinking, the fashion for matching tableware, the advent of forks, the need for sauces for a changing cuisine, all meant a whole magnificent array of table silver for the prosperous merchants and landed gentry. Shapes were still simple, decoration still restrained. Form was based on the cyma curve and the baluster, more curving than the tapering cylindrical shapes of the previous centuries. Candlesticks were still cast in solid silver, and all pieces were of heavier gauge than earlier English silver.

Rococo (*c.*1730-50)
As the century advanced, the shape of silver became more sinuous. Straight spouts vanished in favour of high curved ones, often with heads of animals, handles were scrolled, plain foot rims were replaced with small scrolling feet. With the curves came more ornament: gadrooning and shells, scrolls and foliage, paw feet and lion's masks. Around 1730 these motifs erupted into full-blown rococo, in a fashion which emanated from France, principally from the designs of court silversmith Juste Aurèle Meissonier. Cartouches became assymetrical, there was a return to 'chinoiserie', swirling bases to candlesticks and flambeau finials added to the feeling of movement, so different from the plain and simple lines of Queen Anne silver.

Classical (*c.*1750–1800)
With the return of classicism under the all-pervading influence of the Adam brothers, English silver underwent a radical change. The baluster shape on which so much silver design had been based was swept away in favour of classical urns, vases and columns, decorated with swags and festoons, rams' heads, classical medallions, anthemion, formalised scrolls and leaves. There were helmet-shaped cream jugs and sugar bowls with pedestal feet and swing handles, vase-shaped tea caddies and teapots, all richly engraved with classical themes. Towards the end of the century 'bright cut' engraving produced a more brilliant, almost three-dimensional effect and became the principal method of surface decoration until the end of the century and beyond. Machines for stamping and rolling came into use, resulting in thinner gauge silver for the wider market, and candlesticks were made from stamped sheet metal, wholly or partly, and filled with pitch, known as 'loaded' candlesticks.

Regency (*c.*1800–30)
As with Sheraton furniture, by the end of the 18th century much of the silver made for the general market had been prettified rather than simplified into light and airy shapes and designs, decorated with garlands rather than swags. This tendency was soon to be reversed in favour of the massive, the grand and the sculptural. It was an age which was unsurpassed for craftsmanship and quality, during which many of the massive centrepieces and banqueting services were made which can be seen on display in stately homes today. This was the period of John Flaxman and the great 'Shield of Achilles' manufactured by Rundell, Bridge & Rundell, measuring 36½in/92.71 cm in diameter, and weighing 669 oz 10 dwt and of basins and ewers, sideboard dishes, tureens, entrée dishes and dessert stands embellished with freestanding decoration, cast and applied in spectacular style. The severity of earlier classical shapes gave way to more curving lines, with campana-shaped wine coolers and cisterns and melon-shaped teapots and tea services. Table silver too became much heavier, and to the old relatively plain patterns of Old English,

Hanoverian and traditional rat-tailed patterns were added scrolled heavyweight King's pattern, Queen's pattern and Coburg, amongst others.

Victorian (*c.*1830–1900)
With so much ornament balancing on a knife-edge between the opulent and the vulgar, it was almost inevitable that decline should follow. But although a great deal of silver made during this period was overblown and ostentatious, some extremely fine 'Queen Anne' silver was made, as well as some excellent and original designs which sprang from the Arts & Crafts Movement and Art Nouveau. The period spans so many decades and covers so many changes in manufacturing techniques one should not attempt to generalise. A lot of Victorian silver which looks heavy is in fact made of thin-gauge silver, spun, stamped or embossed by machine, but individual craftsmen were still making fine quality silver with traditional methods, and amongst the proliferation of objects, there is still much to be found of fine workmanship and design.

Edwardian (*c.*1900–20)
There was a little innovation during this period with the exception of some Art Nouveau silver, but many of the reproductions of earlier designs were excellently made in heavy gauge silver by well-established companies such as the Goldsmiths & Silversmiths, Garrards, Mappin & Webb and Aspreys. Dangerous to those who do not know it, is the technique of 'acid-engraving', similar to that used for making plates for printing, and recognizable by its shallow, dull appearance.

Sheffield plate

Sheffield Plate is also known as 'Old Sheffield' and was first made in the 1740s. Thin layers of sterling silver are fused to sheets of copper by heating both metals and then rolling them together. Originally used for making small objects such as buttons, buckles and boxes, once the technique was perfected, almost any item made in silver could be made in Sheffield Plate. From about 1768 silver wire was made by the same process and many really remarkable openwork and wirework epergnes, baskets and sweetmeat dishes were produced which do not have their equivalent in sterling silver. By the last decade of the 18th century it was quite customary for some items of table silver, such as soup tureens, to be accompanied by a stand made of cheaper Sheffield Plate.

The marking of Sheffield Plate however is a quagmire of complications and needs special study and the advice of an expert to be properly understood. It is a subject well worth investigating, for today Sheffield Plate is considerably less expensive than sterling silver and many pieces are every bit as worthy of display.

Electroplating

This process was first patented in 1840 and employed the principal of electrical deposition of gold or silver on to a base metal. Unlike Sheffield Plate, the silver had to be pure, and differs in colour by being bluer and colder than sterling silver. Apart from the fact that this process meant that all kinds of objects could be cast and made in a variety of base metals and then coated in silver, it also made it possible for 'repairs' of a dubious nature to be covered up with a layer of silver – a possibility which fakers and forgers were not slow to realize.

Electrotyping

This is an extension of electroplating, and employs a mould or cast on which the silver is deposited. An extremely costly process, it was used for making very restricted numbers of copies of such famous pieces as John Flaxman's 'Shield of Achilles'. Its merit is that the cast remains as crisp from the first copy to the last, unlike an ordinary cast or mould whose modelling blurs with use.

Marks and hallmarks

Strictly speaking, there is only one actual 'hallmark' on a piece of silver – a leopard's head, crowned or uncrowned, ordained by statute in 1300 when the standard of purity for sterling silver was laid down. But there should be at least four marks on all but the smallest pieces of silver. Apart from the leopard's head there should be a maker's mark, added by law in 1363 and usually the initials of the silversmith, and a date letter, incorporated in 1478. This device, a brilliantly simple way of identifying the Assayer in case of dishonesty or corruption, has become a remarkable and unbroken record, enabling silver to be dated year by year through more than five centuries. The letter changes annually through a twenty year cycle, omitting 'I' and 'V' to 'Z' and each cycle has a different type letter and surround. The London Assay Office began the year in May – provincial offices do not necessarily coincide with London until 1975 when all Assay Offices in Britain agreed to a single date, changed annually on 1 January.

The fourth mark is that of the 'lion passant' and was added in 1544 as a further protection against the adulteration of silver. The various styles of this mark can also help with dating: originally the lion was 'passant guardant' a heraldic term denoting walking with its head turned to regard i.e. full face. The style and surround changed down the centuries and provide a broad indication of period. From 1822 the lion was redesigned in profile but still walking and became simply 'passant'.

In addition to these four marks, between 1784 and 1890 a sovereign's head was added to denote that duty had been paid and these too, apart from the identity of the reigning monarch, add to the verification of authenticity.

If a piece of silver was not made in London but in the provinces, the mark of the provincial assay office will also be struck, as well as the leopard's head in Chester, York, Newcastle and Exeter up to 1777 but not later, and without the leopard's head in Birmingham and Sheffield.

Britannia Standard

One further mark occurs on a limited number of pieces, between the years 1697 and 1720. During this period the standard proportions for silver were changed to increase the pure metal content to 95.8 per cent. It was marked with the figure of Britannia instead of the sterling 'lion passant' and known as 'Britannia Standard'. During those years too, the leopard's head was also removed and a 'lion's head erased' substituted. Another heraldic term meaning a lion's head in profile, with a ragged edge to the neck. The pure silver content is higher and calculations for Britannia Standard is the total weight less 4.2 per cent base metal alloy.

Fakes and forgeries

From 1720 when duty was first imposed even reputable silversmiths transposed marks from a small piece on which tax had really been paid to a larger one to avoid paying duty. These pieces are known as 'duty dodgers' and although at one time illegal, are now bought and collected as oddities in themselves, providing they have been reassayed and found up to sterling standard. Modern fakers and forgers who transpose marks cannot match old silver with new and often resort to electroplating the completed piece with the marks soldered in place in order to conceal the deception. Since electroplating uses pure silver, a simple test will detect this practice: nitric acid slightly diluted with distilled water will turn the surface of sterling silver blue (make the test where it cannot be seen). With pure silver there is no change in colour, therefore it has been electroplated.

Casting up a pair from a genuine single to increase the value can be detected by the fact that every detail including hallmarks are identically placed. In genuine pairs hallmarks never match up in alignment and position.

The common practice of 'improving' silver, thereby reducing its value, was most prevalent in the Victorian era. Plain early silver was embossed and chased with decorative motifs to increase its attraction, and flat-chasing was added to the surface of plain salvers and trays. The removal and addition of armorials is another practice frequently encountered. Probably for reasons of snobbery, old family crests were removed and evidence of 'second hand' silver was thus removed, and a layer of silver with it, thus reducing its value. Newly acquired armorials brashly engraved on pieces of genuine old family silver also reduces the value of a piece.

Provincial, Scottish and Irish Assay Office marks

Birmingham	An anchor.
Chester	A shield with three half-lions and wheatsheaves until 1779: after that three wheatsheaves and a sword.
Dublin	A harp.
Edinburgh	A triple-towered castle.
Exeter	Three towers.
Glasgow	A tree and a salmon.
Newcastle-upon-Tyne	Three towers, two above and one below.
Norwich	A castle above a lion or a crowned Tudor rose, both rare.
Sheffield	A crown, sometimes repeated in the date letter.
York	A cross incorporating five lions.

The various marks would make it seem a simple matter to date and identify a piece of silver, but reading these marks requires considerable skill and knowledge. There is a difference in each cycle of the alphabet, both in the shape of the letter and the surround, often difficult to differentiate. The 'lion passant guardant' changes in design, and so does the leopard's head and the sovereign's head. All the marks must accord, not with wishful thinking, but accurately with the date assumed. Only time and a great deal of experience will provide the ability to read silver marks accurately.

Top A good early 18th century snuff box decorated in Baroque style depicting the Toilet of Venus, probably German. *c.*1820. £400–500.
Above George III silver gilt snuff box with classical scene of the philosopher Diogenes. By Joseph Ash, 1813. 3 in/7.5 cm. £500–600.

Leading silversmiths

Angell, Joseph 1811–24 and son John Angell 1824–*c.*1850. Well-known maker of tea and coffee sets.

Barnard, Emes & Barnard 1808–29. Messrs. Barnard from 1829. High quality ware, and many important table centrepieces and cups.

Bateman, Hester 1761–90. Domestic silver of high quality, with the workshop continuing with Peter and Jonathon, Ann, William and William II.

Boulton, Matthew Birmingham metalworker and silversmith, in association with John Fothergill, and with many leading designers, making high quality silverware, Sheffield plate and ormolu from 1784, the business continued until 1819.

Cafe, John Specialist candlestick maker from 1740–57, followed by his brother William until *c.*1775.

Chawner, Henry 1786–1810. High quality silverware, especially teapots and tea ware, in partnership with John Emes 1796–1810.

Coker, Ebenezer 1738–*c.*1780. Candlestick maker, salvers and chambersticks.

de Lamerie, Paul 1713–51. The most famous London silversmith, particularly associated with rococo style, as well as more simple items.

Elkington & Co. Birmingham. Famous makers in 19th century, probably best known for electrotyping and electroplating.

Emes, John. In partnership with Barnard, see above.

Farrell, Edward 1813–35. Copyist of early styles and maker of typically-associated florid Victorian wares.

Fogelberg, Andrew *c.*1770–*c.*1800. Master of Paul Storr.

Fox, Charles son of Charles Fox I working *c.*1822–*c.*1840. Produced many items associated with the Dutch style, workshop continued with George Fox until *c.*1860.

Garrard, Robert 1792–1818. Good quality silverware, the business continuing with his son Robert II from 1818–53.

Gould, James 1722–47. Candlestick maker, as well as his son William 1732–56.

Hennell, Robert 1763–1811. One of a large dynasty of silvermakers, including his father David, and sons David Hennell II and Samuel, and grandson Robert, working until 1868.

Hunt & Roskell. A 19th-century workshop producing work of famous designers such as Paul Storr, Flaxman.

Platel, Pierre 1697–1719. Huguenot silversmith famous for work of highest quality, master of Paul de Lamerie who was his apprentice.

Scofield 1776–96. One of the finest silversmiths of his period, making fine quality designs of great craftsmanship.

Smith, Benjamin 1802–18. Designed and worked almost exclusively for Rundell, Bridge and Rundell, making work of extremely high quality.

Storr, Paul 1792–1838. Maker and designer of sumptuous high quality silver, for Rundell, Bridge and Rundell as well as more delicate items.

Willaume, David 1697–1728. Huguenot silversmith working in England, the business continuing with his son David Willaume II from 1728–*c.*1746.

Wood, Samuel 1733–*c.*1773. Specialist caster maker.

Commonwealth sweetmeat dish with scalloped handles and punched decoration. *c.*1654. 6⅛in / 15.5 cm diameter. £800–1000.

Commonwealth wine taster with looped wire handles and punched pineapple decoration. *c.*1655. 4¾in / 12 cm diameter. £700–900.

Charles II beaker with embossed and flat-chased decoration and applied foot-rim. 1683. 5½in / 14 cm high. £1500–2500.

Charles II bleeding bowl with cast pierced handle, possibly by William Gamble 1682. 5⅜in / 14 cm diameter. £1500–2500.

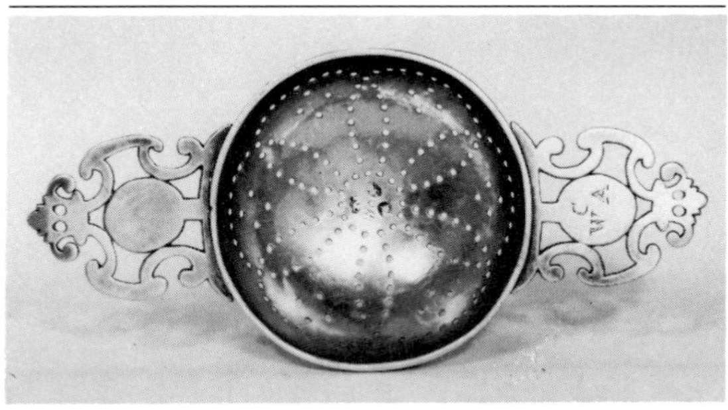

George I two-handled lemon strainer by Thomas Keddon. 1715. £800–1100.

Commonwealth porringer and cover with tulip and bead punched decoration, capstan top and cast handles in the shape of fish. 1657. 3¾ in/9.5 cm high. £4000–6000.

Charles II porringer embossed and chased with lion and unicorn with flowerheads and cast handles. 1683. 3¾ in/9.5 cm high. £2500–4000.

William III two-handled porringer with gadrooned decoration by Robert Timbrell 1703. £1200–2500.

George I casters of octagonal baluster shape with engraved armorials, one pierced, one blind. 6½ in / 16 cm high.
Pair: £1200–1800.
Single: £750–1000.

Queen Anne sugar caster of baluster form with applied girdle, pierced decoration and bayonet fitting by Christopher Canner I. 1707. 8 in / 20.5 cm high.
£1200–1500.

Left George II caster of baluster shape and rococo design by Samuel Wood. 1758. 2½ in / 6 .25 cm.
£450–750.

A pair of 19th-century casters with applied girdles and vineleaves by Elkington & Co. 7 in / 18 cm high.
£800–1000. (Heavy gauge)

George III oval salts with ramsheads, swags and beaded rims by Robert Hennell II. 1777. £500–800.

William IV salts with cast shell feet by Edward Farrell. 1833. 2¾in/7cm diameter. Pair: £250–300.

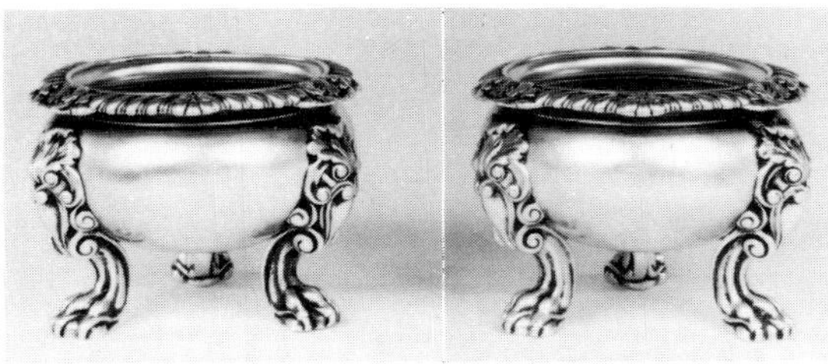

George III salts with cast paw feet and gadrooned rims by John Bridge. 1824. Pair: £550–750.

Victorian salts in the shape of shells on dolphin supports and seawave bases, after the style of Paul Storr. Pair: £2000–3000. Single: £1200–1800.

George II cream pitcher with applied cast handle, possibly by Jonathan Newton. 1736. 3 in/7.5 cm. £500–850.

George III baluster cream jug with double-scroll handle and reverse bead punched border by Hester Bateman. 1785. £350–400.

George III cream jug with moulded pleated sides and reeded border by Peter and Anne Bateman. 1798. £150–200.

George III helmet-shaped cream jug with bright-cut decoration by Thos. Wallis II. 1802. £200–300.

George II sauce boat with wavy-cut border and cast shell-and-hoof feet by William Skeen. 1759. Pair: £1200–1800.

Below right George III sauce boat with gadrooned rim, cast shell feet and leaf-capped scroll handle by Smith & Sharpe. 1762. Pair: £1200–2000.

Above George III sauce boat with cast shell feet, gadrooned border and acanthus leaf handle by Fuller & Unite. 1761. Pair: £1000–1500.

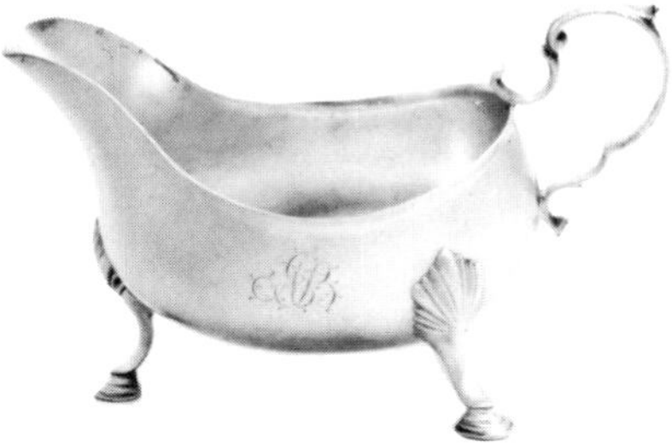

George III Irish butter boat with shell-and-hoof feet and cast double scroll handle by Charles Townsend. Dublin 1775. Pair: £2000–2750 Single: £400–500.

George III Scottish chamberstick with plain circular pan and flying scroll handle by William Drummond. Edinburgh 1767. £750–900.

A pair of George III chambersticks and extinguisher caps with gadrooned shell and foliate borders and openwork stems for snuffers by Samuel Hennell and John Terry. 1814. 4in/11.4cm high. Pair: £1000–1600.

George IV chamberstick with gadroon shell and foliate border, matching decoration to drip pan and extinguisher cap with ornate flying scroll handle, openwork stem for snuffers and rounded urn-shaped sconce by Matthew Boulton & Co. 1823. Pair: £1200–1850.

Chamberstick with deep dished pan and pierced gallery with S-scrolls with loop handle by Ramsden & Carr. 1912. £800–1200.

James II cast candlesticks with canted corners, baluster turned with reeded stems. 1688. 6¼in/15.9cm high. Pair: £5000–8000.

George II cast candlesticks with wavy-pleated bases, ribbed drip-pans and shoulder knops by John Cafe. 1749. 7¾in/19.7cm high. Pair: £2600–3000.

George II cast candlesticks with chased shells and swirls with leaf decoration to shoulder knop, with loaded bases by James Gould. 1744/5. 8½in/22cm high. Pair: £1800–2400.

George II cast candlesticks with shell bases and engraved armorial lozenge, shell decoration to drip-pans and flared shoulder knops by Simon Jouet *c.*1755. 8½in/22cm high. Pair: £2600–3000.

George III tapersticks with square bases and acanthus leaf decoration, gadrooned shoulder knops and stamped decoration to drip-pans *c.*1770. 7¼in / 18.4cm high. Pair: £2500–4500.

George III candlesticks in embossed sheet silver, baluster-shaped with heavy rococo decoration in high relief by John and Thomas Settle. Sheffield 1816. Pair: £1000–1500. Loaded.

George IV candlesticks with flared shoulder knops and vestigial leaf decoration to the baluster base by S.C. Younge & Co. Sheffield 1829. Pair: £1000–1400. Loaded.

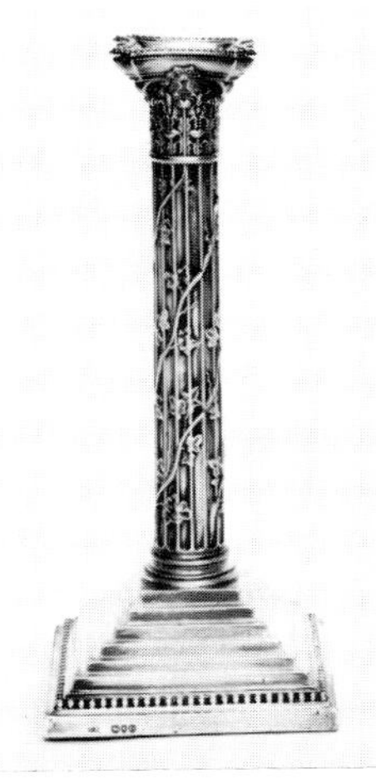

Late Victorian candlesticks based on Adam-style Corinthian column with high-stepped bases and entwined ivy up the stem, by Charles Boyton, 1891. Pair: £1000–1350. Loaded.

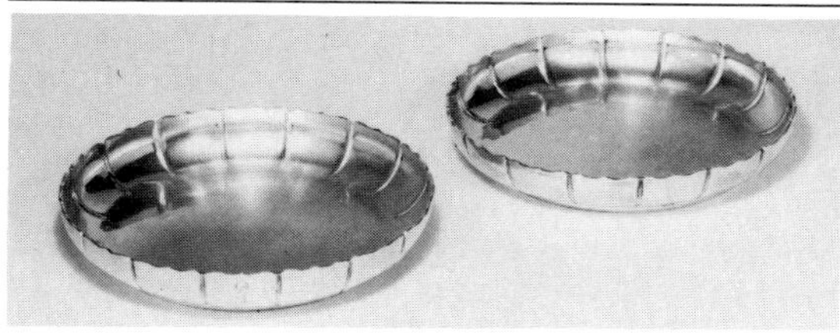

A pair of strawberry dishes with fluted sides and scalloped rims with engraved armorial on the outer rim, of a shape and style dating from mid-18th century, but late Georgian by John & Edward Edwards. 1814/15. £1000–1500.

Oval meat dish with gadroon and leaf border, the most typical shape, usually made to match sets of plates, from early Georgian to Victorian. 1821. £700–1000.

Set of standard pattern dinner plates of mixed Victorian and Edwardian dates, with plain gadrooned borders and scalloped edges marked for 1839, 1849 and 1904. Half dozen: £3500–4800.

Set of soup plates of similar design with shallower gadrooning round the rims. 1849. Half dozen: £3200–4400.

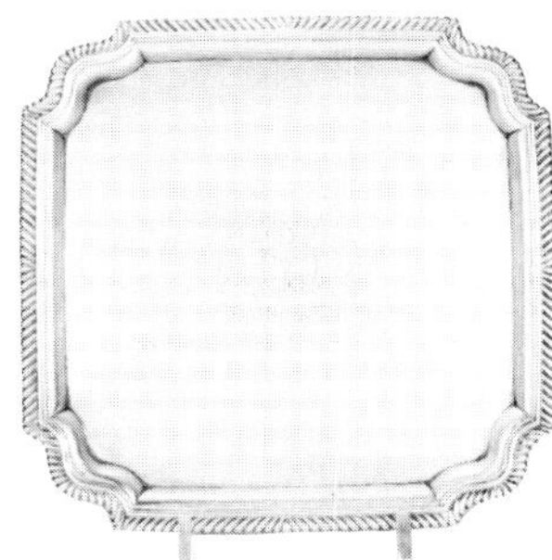

Above A pair of George I tazza on plain foot with finely engraved cartouche in the style of the period by William Gamble 1718. 10⅜ in / 26.4 cm diameter. £4000–5000. Single: £1500–1800.

Left: George II octafoil salver with gadrooned border, mounted on plain cast feet, by Louis Cuny. 1733. 9 in / 22.9 cm wide. £3250–4250.

Above left George III Irish oval salver with reeded border and cast fluted feet by Richard Sawyer, Dublin 1799. 12½ in / 32 cm across. £1900–2250. *Above right* George II salver with forward and reverse scroll and shell border on cast scroll feet by William Justis. 1750. £4250–6000.

Victorian salver with rococo-style shell and scroll border and flat-chased base with rocaille motif on cast shell feet by William Eley II. 1839. 11¼ in / 28.5 cm diameter. £600–900.

George III cake basket with pierced panels interspersed with beaded flutes, with cast applied rococo foot, bead and shell supports to the lattice-pierced swing handle and gadroon and leaf border by William Plummer. 1761. 14½in/36.8cm long. £1250–2300.

Flared oval cake basket on plain reeded foot, decorated with bright-engraving around the rim and a plain reeded swing-handle probably by Robert Jones. 1795. 13⅜in/34cm long. £1000–1500.

A pair of Victorian wine coolers, modelled as wooden pails with two ribbons around the sides, complete with liners, by Elkington & Co. 1873. 8½in/22cm high. £600–1000.

William IV cake basket of circular form with pleated sides embossed and chased with flowers and foliage on pleated foot with applied cast border, and a pierced stem and flower swing handle by E., E.J. & W. Barnard. 1832. 13¼in/33.6cm diameter. £650–1000.

William III monteith with detachable scalloped rim engraved husk decoration gadrooned cartouches, and lion's mask handles on circular gadrooned foot by Charles Overing. London 1701. 11 in/27.9 cm diameter. £7000–10000.

Right Late Victorian monteith with moulded girdle, lobed decoration and spreading lobed foot, the applied rim taken from the early design of above. 1893. 12¾ in/32.5 cm diameter. £900–1200.

Left George I circular punch-bowl with applied wire rim and spreading foot by William Paradise. 1723. 8⅔ in/22 cm. £3000–4500.

Right Victorian rose-bowl with moulded flutes and rococo-style cartouche on moulded decorated foot, chased and embossed by Charles Stuart Harris. 1896. 9⅝ in/24.5 cm diameter. £650–1250.

George II soup tureen and cover with embossed gadroon and foliate decoration with pomegranate finial and cast rococo scroll feet and handles, with engraved armorial by Samuel Courtauld I. 1759. £12 500–15 500.

A pair of covered vegetable dishes with moulded pleats and rolled scrolls and scroll loop handles by Paul Storr. 1835. 13½ in/34 cm across. £15 000–20 000.

Soup tureen with gadroon and leaf decoration, heavy cast scroll and foliate handles and applied feet with engraved armorial by John Hunt. 1851. 16 in/41 cm long. £5000–7000.

A pair of Victorian entrée dishes and covers with gadroon and foliate decoration, removable shell and scroll handles and applied decoration. *c.* 1850. 11¼ in/29 cm long. £2500–3500.

Charles II tankard on spreading circular foot with applied foot rim, single stepped lid, S-scroll handle and bifurcated billet or thumbpiece. London 1664. 7⅛ in / 18 cm high. £5500–7500.

Right George III baluster-shaped tankard with applied reeded girdle, S-scroll handle, domed lid and shell billet or thumbpiece, possibly by John Scofield. 1776. 7½ in / 18.5 cm high. £1500–2000.

George III tankard with tapering shape, high domed lid, applied reeded girdle and skirted base by Godbehere & Wigan. 1787. 8 in / 20.5 cm high. £900–1200.

George III tankard with domed, reeded lid, applied girdle. S-scroll handle and 'chairback' pierced billet. 1791. 8 in / 20.5 cm high. £950–1350.

Queen Anne mug of very simple form with reeded rim and applied reeded foot rim and simple scrolling handle by Thomas Parr I. 1713. 4¼ in / 11 cm high. £500–700.

Left George II mug of baluster form with tuck-in body and applied foot rim, with simple scrolling handle. *c.*1731. 5 in / 13 cm high. £400–500.

George III mug of baluster shape with spreading circular foot and double scroll handle with leaf capping. *c.*1761. 5½ in / 14 cm high. £350–500.

Victorian christening mug with elaborately embossed and chased romantic scene in a floral panel and double scroll handle by Francis Higgins. 1861. £300–400.

Charles I wine goblet with engraved simple armorial and punched date '1639' of slightly tapering shape with cast baluster stem and spreading foot. Maker's mark 'W.R.' London, *c.*1635. 5 in/12.7 cm high. £3000–5000.

George III goblet with slender stem and beaded circular foot, with bright-engraved decoration of swags and flowers by Walter Brind. 1784. 6½ in/16.5 cm high. Pairs: £1000–1500. Single: £400–650.

George III wine goblet of oval shape with turned baluster stem and beaded knops, with beaded circular foot, by Charles Wright. 1777/8. 6½ in/16.5 cm high. Pairs: £1200–1800. Single: £400–500.

Victorian wine goblet with heavy foliate engraved decoration, beaded collars to slender stem and punched circular foot by William Eaton. 1872. £200–250.

George III vase-shaped ewer with beaded borders, ebonised fruitwood handle, engraved armorial and cast pineapple finial by John Scofield. 1778.
13 in / 32.5 cm high.
£950–1450.

Victorian **plated** claret jug with raised pedestal foot, beaded rim and frieze embossed with acanthus and moulded neck girdle. *c.*1870.
13⅜ in / 34 cm high.
£200–250.

A pair of Victorian silver-mounted claret jugs with baluster-shaped bodies etched with stars, with embossed and engraved silver mounts, beaded girdle at the base of the neck and bifurcated scroll handles by W. & G. Sissons. Sheffield 1869.
£1200–1800.

Late Victorian **plated** claret jugs with mask spouts, embossed mounts decorated with vines and masks on a matted background, with lion finials. *c.* 1890. Pair: £500–600.

George III wine coasters with pierced sides with Vitruvian scroll decoration and urns by Robert Hennell. 1777. Pair: £1000–1500.

Victorian wine coasters in cast metal in rococo revival style with chased scrollwork and armorial on the bases, by E., E.J. & W. Barnard. 1841. Pair: £1400–1750.

A matched pair of George III coasters, the sides pierced with fruiting vines, one by Benjamin and James Smith, 1811, the other by Benjamin Smith, 1814. 5⅞ in/13.7 cm diam. £1500–1600.

George III fox's mask stirrup cups with gilt interiors by Tudor & Leader, *c.* 1780. 5 in/13 m long. £2000–3000 each.

a Three Elaborate Bacchanalian wine labels with putti, grapes and vine leaves *c.*1745. £300–450. **b** Three Victorian wine labels. £200–300. **c** Six Georgian plain wine labels with wavy edges. £500–600. **d** Six Victorian vine-leaf wine labels. £480–550. **e** Five 18th-century Georgian wine labels chased with vine leaves. £250–300.

George III pear-shaped coffee pot with gadrooned rim and foot, cast scrolled applied spout, flame finial and ebonised fruitwood handle with fine period armorials, by Whipham & Wright. 1761. 10½in/27cm high.
£2000–3000.

George III baluster coffee pot with decorative knop finial, scalloped spout, scrolled ebonised fruitwood handle with shell mount, possibly by Fuller White 1765. 10½in/27cm high.
£1200–1600.

Right George III baluster-shaped coffee pot on pedestal foot with high domed lid and acorn finial, cast scrolled animalier spout, scrolled ebonised fruitwood handle with shell and scroll mounts by John Langlands. Newcastle *c.*1790. 10¾in/27.5cm high. £1200–1900.

George III coffee pot with gadrooned rim and spreading foot with cast scrolled animalier spout, pineapple finial, domed lid and ebonised fruitwood handle with scroll and shell mounts probably by John Scofield. 1775.
11in/28.2cm high.
£1800–2200.

George III urn-shaped coffee pot with beaded borders, high domed lid with urn finial, beaded decoration to the cast applied spout and heavy reeded mounts to the handle by Langlands & Robertson. 1784. 12¾in/32cm high. £1600–2200.

George III coffee biggin with lobed base and decoration with ivory or bone handle by Alice and George Burrows. 1813. 8½in/21.5cm high. £500–700.

Above George III coffee pot on tall pedestal base with thin gadrooned borders and sweeping ebonised handle by William Abdy. 1803. 11¼in/28.6cm high. £600–800.

Left Victorian reproduction of side-handled 18th-century coffee pot of 'Queen Anne' style with lidded spout, tapered shape and scrolled billet. 9¾in/24.8cm high. £800–1000.

George III kettle-on-stand, the hob-shaped kettle with raffia-bound swing handle and small acanthus decoration, the triangular plain stand on flattened paw feet. Lamp marked Wakelin & Taylor. 1782. 14¼in/36.19cm high. £1250–1850.

Squat-shaped Victorian kettle-on-stand with chased foliate decoration, flower finial and C-scroll mounts to plain silver handle with ivory collars, the pierced openwork stand with shells and scrolls, on four scrolling feet, by Charles Reilly and George Storer. 1843. £900–1400.

Flattened pear-shaped tea-kettle with elaborate chased and embossed floral decoration, the animalier spout with mask, C-scroll mounts to silver handle and solid base on scrolled paw feet, by Elkington & Co. 1846. 13in/33cm overall. £1600–2400.

Edwardian kettle-on-stand with chased decoration, double scroll mounts to stained ivory handle, the stand pierced and decorated with flowers, on S-scroll and flattened shell feet. By Goldsmiths & Silversmiths Company. *c.*1909. 13⅜in/34cm high. £780–1125.

Queen Anne teapot of small capacity with octagonal curved spout cast in two halves and applied, with high-domed lid, stand-away hinge and ebonised handle. 1717. 4½in/11.5cm high. £3500–5000.

George II bullet teapot with decorative engraving round the shoulder, flush-fitting lid, cast and applied spout and carved scrolled ivory handle. *c.*1735. 5¼in/13.5cm high. £1500–2500.

George III provincial drum-shaped teapot with beaded borders, flush hinge to lid, plain turned finial and ebonised wooden handle. Newcastle 1802. 5¼in/13.5cm. £750–1100.

George III oval drum-shaped teapot with bright-cut engraved decoration of floral swags and staved border, with flat stepped lid, flush hinge, plain ebonised finial and sweeping handle, with original reeded stand on small cast feet, by Alexander Field. 1800. Teapot height 5¼in/13.5cm. £850–1250.

George III teapot and stand with fluted sides and oval shape, curved shallow domed lid, plain ebonised finial and handle. *c.*1780. £750–1250.

William IV teapot with melon-shaped body and lid, on small scrolling cast shell feet. Profuse floral and leaf decoration to the body and cast spout and a silver handle which has ivory collars, by Charles Goodwinor and Charles Gordon. 1832. 6⅝in/17m high. £400–500.

Victorian teapot of squat pear-shape with segmented fluted sides and domed lid with spiral finial, diaper and bead decoration, and silver handle with ivory collars by Emes & Barnard. 1862. 6¼in/16cm high. £450–850.

Reproduction 'Queen Anne' teapot with domed lid and plain finial, applied plain foot and rim and silver handle with ivory collars, made throughout the Victorian period. 4¾in/12cm high. £450–750.

William IV tea and coffee set in standard popular melon-shape with open-flower finials, and cast decorative feet, the tea and coffee pots both with silver handles and ivory collars, made by different silversmiths and made up from different sets 1815–38. £1250–1750.

Victorian four-piece tea and coffee set in elaborate and popular '*Louis Quatorze*' pattern with rococo cartouche, on small scrolled cast and applied feet, with winged finials by D. & H. Houle. 1857. £1650–2200.

Victorian tea and coffee set of panelled shape on stepped pedestal bases and with engraved swags and oval cartouches and curving spouts, the tea and coffee pots have silver handles with ivory collars, helmet jug and swing handled sugar basket by Elkington & Co. 1873. £1000–1200.

Victorian 'bachelor's' tea set with tapering square sides decorated with Japanese scenes by E. C. Brown. 1876. £600–900.

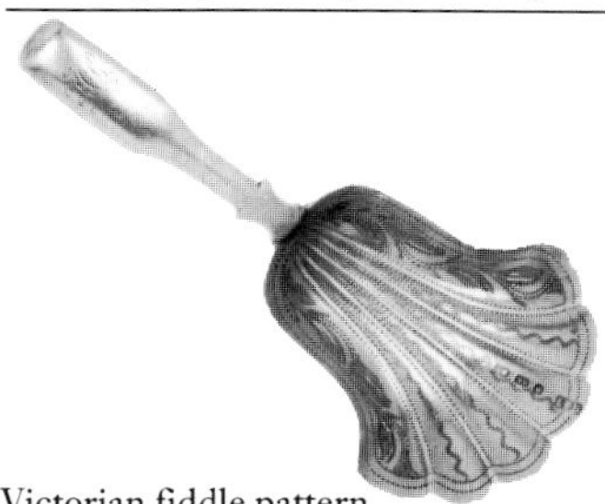

Victorian fiddle pattern spoon with flared fluted bowl by Hilliard & Thomason. Birmingham 1862. £80–120.

Victorian parcel gilt spoon with handle in the form of coiled stem and lily pad, the bowl as three waterlilies and a rocaille bowl. Birmingham 1856. £200–280.

George IV shovel-shaped bowl with fiddle pattern handle, maker's mark overstruck Richard John Bilton. 1827. £80–100.

Victorian bell-shaped parcel gilt spoon embossed with grapes and coiled vines, probably Birmingham 1850. £80–100.

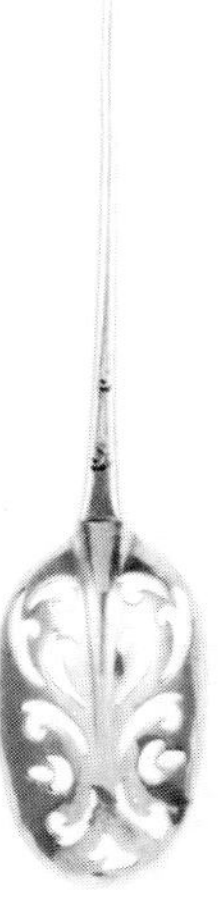

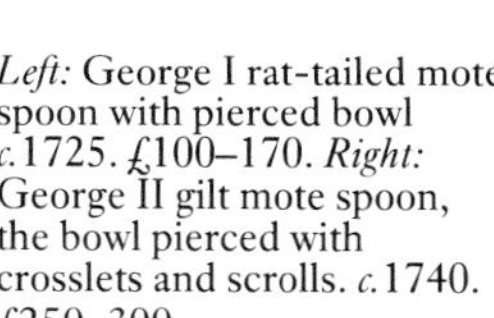

Left: George I rat-tailed mote spoon with pierced bowl *c.*1725. £100–170. *Right:* George II gilt mote spoon, the bowl pierced with crosslets and scrolls. *c.*1740. £250–300.

Charles I sealtop spoon *c.*1640. 7in/17.8cm. £450–650.

William III trefid spoon initialled 'MM' London 1698. £250–300.

James I apostle spoon of St. Matthew, London 1611. £420–580.

George III bright-cut spoons, Old English pattern engraved with contemporary initials, Hester Bateman 1787. Six £300–400.

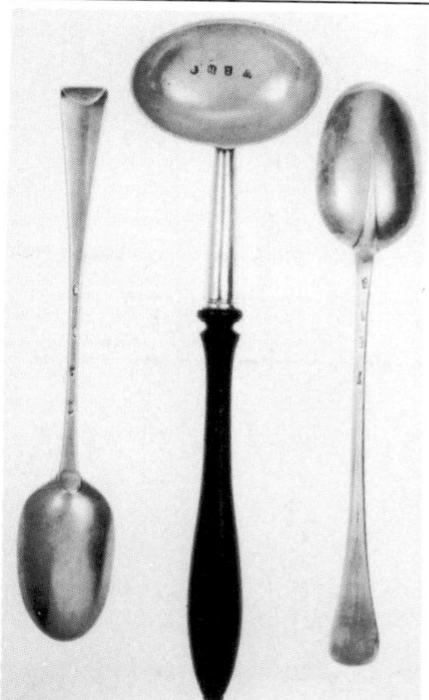

Above centre George II punch ladle. London 1737. £250–500. *Left* George III Irish gravy spoon, Old English pattern with turn-over end, possibly by Alexander Richards. Dublin 1761. £275–400. *Right* Queen Anne basting spoon with rat-tail and egg-shaped bowl 1710. £300–600.

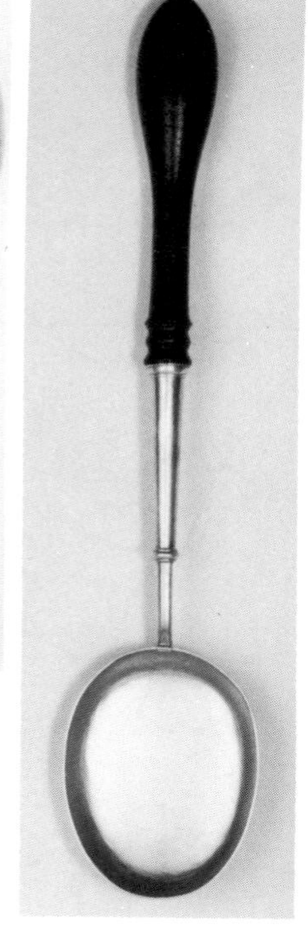

George II basting spoon with turned wood handle by Isaac Cookson. Newcastle 1748. £300–400.

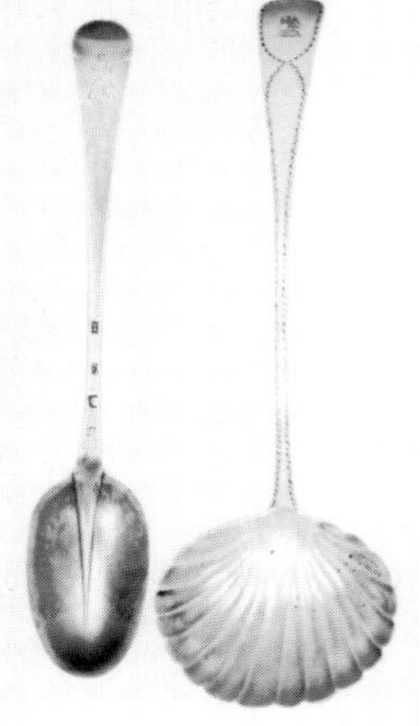

Left George I basting spoon with rat-tail engraved with contemporary initials by Richard Scarlett. London 1722. £275–500. *Right* William IV soup ladle with scalloped bowl and bright-cut decoration. Dublin 1834. £120–210.

Above Canteen of late Victorian Old English pattern by George Adams. London 1888. £2000–2800.

Canteen of Victorian and modern mixed makers, Prince's pattern. £2270–3100.

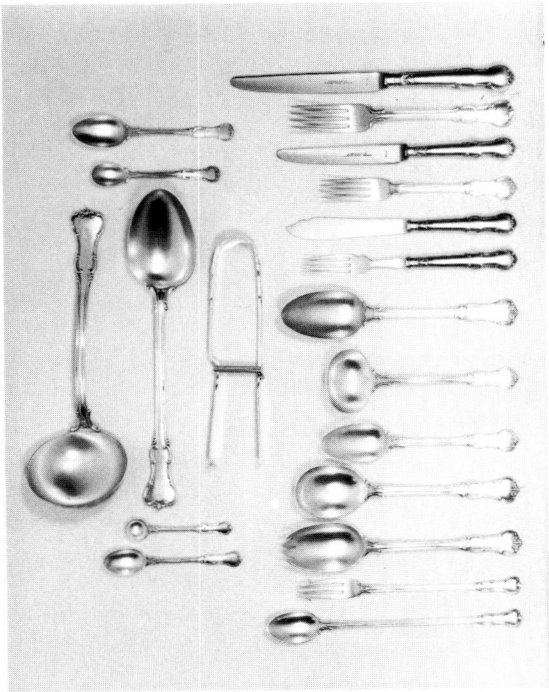

Modern canteen of 12 places of rat-tail pattern with bone-handled knives. £2850–3850.

Canteen of 12 places of plain tapering ribbed pattern similar to 'Athlone'. £3000–4000.

Top left A late 17th century spice box, of oblong shape with rounded ends, engraved with flowers and with squeeze-action sides, maker's mark only possibly IB. 1¾in / 4½cm. *c.*1680. £300–400.
Centre left An oval Paktong snuff box, the cover decorated in relief with a Topers scene after Tenniers, probably 18th century. £300–400.
Bottom left An early 19th century Russian niello snuff box, with architectural views of Moscow on the cover and base, and similar decoration around the sides, maker's mark FL (Cyrillics). *c.*1828. £300–400.
Top right An 18th century French boîte-à-mouche, of tortoiseshell lacquered in a plum colour, with gold mounts, the cover applied with an oval enamel plaque of a fruit seller sitting inside her house beside baskets of her produce, the interior with three compartments, two with small hinged covers and set in the cover with a mirror. *c.*1770. £700–800.
Centre right A Russian cloisonné enamel cigarette case, decorated with geometric designs in red, white and four shades of blue, probably by Gustav Klingert, Moscow. *c.*1890. £300–400.
Bottom right An attractive George II gold mounted mocha agate snuff box of cartouche shape chased with flowers. *c.*1745. £700–800.

American vesta case *c.* 1870. £50–80.

Vesta case with Mr. Punch's dog *c.* 1890. £50–80.

American vesta case with Red Indian head *c.* 1880. £70–90.

Victorian scent bottle shaped as an owl. £40–60.
18th century scent bottle with cut star-pattern glass, open-hinged lid with coronet and initials. £90–120.

Pottery and Porcelain

This is a long-established field for the specialist and the collector, and has been ever since precious pieces of Oriental porcelain first came into England in the 17th century. Porcelain was displayed on shelves of court cupboards, buffets, side cupboards and cabinets from that time onwards, the fashion being so well-established that 18th-century potteries made 'cabinet ware' specifically to be admired but never used.

Recognition

For the first-time buyer or the early days of collecting the most important factor is the ability to distinguish between the different stages in the development of English pottery and porcelain and to know in general terms which potteries and porcelain factories manufactured the various kinds of ware. English pottery and porcelain, for reasons which will become clear, developed along rather different lines from their European counterparts, and have therefore not been separated into two distinct categories in this section. Instead, the two have been put into roughly chronological order of development, since in England stoneware continued to be refined and improved at the same time as the finer-bodied porcelains were developed.

While this is obviously a simplified approach to such a highly-specialized field, it is important to have a firm grasp on the essential differences and simultaneous developments of both pottery and porcelain since, apart from anything else, they have a direct bearing on value and price.

Differences and drawbacks

The principal aim of all European potters was to imitate, if not to reproduce, the fine Oriental porcelain which came into England in the 17th century through the Dutch and English East India Companies. 'True porcelain', however, is chemically different from any pottery or stoneware. It is a combination of kaolin clay and china stone or petuntse, both geologically related to granite. In fine powder form these two substances are formed into a paste and left to mature, a process which gives it such remarkable strength and translucency. It was then worked, allowed to dry until it resembled the consistency of leather, and then fired once before being glazed and fired again at a considerably higher temperature.

The first imitation of Oriental ware in Europe was Delft – earthenware glazed with a white tin enamel and then decorated with Chinese motifs. It was a passable imitation to look at, but it was coarse, heavy, porous and not resistant to hot water and therefore could not be used for making tea pots, a coveted item imported from the East. In *c.*1684 a fine salt-glazed stoneware was developed in England which was both light in weight, non-porous and resistant to hot water – a 'body' which was made and used by many early potteries for making tea and coffee ware.

By *c.*1710 the German factory of Meissen succeeded in making 'true' or hard-paste porcelain and soon other European factories acquired the secrets of its manufacture. Failure of the English potteries was not due to any lack of effort or skill. All ceramics are made from geological deposits of clay and minerals, and Britain was not richly endowed with the materials essential for making hard-paste porcelain. The refinement and improvement of all the various stonewares were a direct result of this lack of raw material. Even when 'soft-paste porcelain' was discovered by the Bow factory in the 1750s it was not heat-resistant, and so the parallel development of stoneware continued in the attempt to bring it closer in substance and appearance to 'true' porcelain. At the same time, porcelain factories experimented with additives to increase the strength of soft-paste porcelain in order to make it hot-water resistant.

Parallel development

Salt-glazed stoneware, while remaining eminently suitable for tea and coffee pots, was not very satisfactory for 'useful wares' since it was fragile and cracked and broke easily with handling. A more satisfactory and durable ware was first produced commercially around 1750 by Josiah Wedgwood, using a liquid cream-coloured glaze over a refined, lighter-coloured body which was fired at a lower temperature than salt-glazed stoneware. It too, failed to be heat-resistant in its early stages, but from the 1760s the problem had been solved and tea and coffee wares were made in addition to a wide variety of table ware.

Although it could be said that throughout the 18th century the original inspiration for English potters remained unchanged – to emulate Chinese porcelain – by the middle of the 18th century European porcelain was in great demand and English factories began to imitate the wares of Sèvres, Meissen, Dresden and other famous Continental makers, while continuing to improve and refine their own products. Bow experimented with the addition of bone ash to soft paste to strengthen it and make it heat resistant, while other manufacturers used a variety of different additives, of which felspar and soapstone were probably the most widely and successfully used. Many useful wares were made by the now-famous English porcelain factories in soapstone porcelain while they continued to make cabinet ware and decorative ornaments in soft-paste porcelain.

Meanwhile the manufacturers of stoneware were constantly experimenting and improving their wares, using vitreous additives and firing them at very high temperatures, improving glazes and developing all kinds of new techniques for painting, enamelling and decorating, so that their products too came closer and closer to the elusive 'true' porcelain and to the marvellously intricate and decorative wares being made on the Continent. In this field the name Wedgwood recurs again and again as he developed and produced first his successful creamware, then a distinctive yellow glaze and a green glaze, and all manner of different stoneware, including black basaltes, jasper ware, cane ware, piecrust ware and bamboo ware. In 1779 he produced an improvement of his creamware called 'pearlware' which proved eminently suitable for transfer-printing and was quickly adopted for the mass market.

'True' porcelain or hard-paste porcelain was only made in England by three potteries: Plymouth, Bristol and New Hall, from about 1768, and production virtually ceased commercially after Spode began producing 'bone china' in 1794. Although the production of hard-paste porcelain was a considerable achievement, it must be said that many of the results lacked refinement, particularly some of the copies of Dresden figures which were clumsily executed because of the problems experienced in working with this difficult medium.

Some technicalities

Glazes perform a dual function: they impart to the body a desirable glassy finish, and they render porous bodies waterproof. Pigments, paints and enamels were either applied to the body which had been fired once, when it is known as 'biscuit' or painted on after the glaze had been fired. These are the most common terms which occur in conjunction with pottery and porcelain:

Slip-glazing

Earthenware was dipped into a liquid glaze the consistency of cream and then fired in a kiln so that the glaze fused to the body. Decoration was done before firing by combing, scraping or trailing a coloured glaze over the article. Colours were limited, usually ochre-yellows, dark brown or white because pigments were little understood.

Tin glazing, tin enamelling

Earthenware was fired first, then coated with a layer of glaze which sunk into the porous body, then decorated, usually with cobalt blue, sometimes with yellow, less commonly with manganese, green, puce. It was then fired a second time, fusing both glaze and decoration to the body and producing a clear white glassy finish. It was not very serviceable for everyday use however, and plates and dishes tended to be used seldom, and more often displayed.

Salt-glaze

A method of imparting a glassy finish to stoneware by adding salt to the kiln at maximum heat, when it volatilised and fused to the clay. Decoration was added afterwards in paint or enamel.

Underglaze decoration

Colour and pattern painted on to a once-fired body in a limited palette since only a few pigments were suitable, then covered in transparent glaze and fired again. Underglaze decoration was used on soft-paste porcelain and a number of light-coloured pottery bodies.

Blue underglaze
Developed in association with transfer printing by Robert Hancock of Worcester, improved at Caughley and perfected by Spode *c.*1780, on a refined stoneware body. The design was transferred on to the once-fired body, fired again, then covered in transparent glaze and fired a third time.

Overglaze decoration
Decoration applied over the glaze of soft-paste porcelain and its variations, using 'cold' pigments, i.e. not fired again and therefore liable to flake and wear.

Enamelled colours
Overglaze decoration of soft-paste porcelain, soapstone porcelain and other variations, using pigments combined with a lead oxide glaze which were then fired again. A difficult process technically, and not always successful. From *c.*1812 coloured enamels were fired in a muffle kiln which made the process more reliable and the colours more brilliant.

Bat printing
A form of transfer-printing over the glaze as opposed to underglaze. Limited use from about 1780, more common after *c.*1825.

Gilding
One of the earliest methods was oil gilding with gold leaf. Discarded in favour of improved, more durable techniques by many potteries by the mid-18th century, it was still in use in Staffordshire until *c.*1790. Japanned gilding, also with gold leaf, was fired and burnished. In use from *c.*1740 it was more lasting than oil gilding. Honey gilding, literally grinding gold leaf with honey, was used from *c.*1755. It was duller in appearance but more lasting and could be burnished. Mercury gilding was not used in England until the late 1780s, though widely applied on the Continent. The results are less soft in tone, more yellow and metallic. From the beginning of the 19th century, techniques multiplied into a diversity of methods, including transfer gilding, underglaze gilding and acid gilding.

Principal potteries and dating pottery and porcelain

Marks are incised, impressed, painted or printed. These distinctions are helpful in the dating and authenticity of pieces.

Belleek Parian, porcelain and earthenware, from *c.*1863. Impressed or relief moulded *c.*1863–90. Printed mark *c.*1863–91.

Bow Soft-paste porcelain 1745–75. Early marks incised or impressed *c.*1750–60. Painted anchor and dagger on figure and groups from *c.*1760. Blue crescent mark, as on Worcester, Caughley and Lowestoft porcelain.

Bristol Unmarked tin-glazed delft-type earthenware to *c.*1750. Hard-paste porcelain from *c.*1770–81. Painted cross or letter B. Crossed-swords 'Dresden' mark in underglaze blue 1770–81.

Caughley Soapstone porcelain from *c.*1775–99. Blue painted or printed 'S' mark, often with small cross or circle on underglaze blue *c.*1775–95. Printed and painted 'C' sometimes mistaken for Worcester crescent mark *c.*1775–95. Blue printed crescent mark occasionally on blue painted articles *c.*1775–95.

Chelsea Soft-paste porcelain 1745–69. Incised triangle mark *c.*1745–50. Rare raised anchor mark *c.*1749–52. Red anchor mark painted *c.*1752–56. Gold anchor mark *c.*1756–69.

Coalport Hard-paste porcelain type *c.*1795–1820. Felspar porcelain *c.*1822–50. Impressed numeral '2' on plates 1805–25. Rare mark in underglaze blue on willow-pattern type designs *c.*1810–20. Large printed mark 1820–30. Printed mark 'John Rose & Co.' *c.*1830–50. Painted or gilt monogram *c.*1851–61.

Copeland Earthenware, parian and porcelain 1847–1970. Rare printed mark *c.*1847–51. Standard printed mark *c.*1851–85. Standard printed marks for earthenware: W. T. Copeland, Copeland and late Spode.

Davenport Earthenware, porcelain *c.*1793–1887. Impressed marks on earthenware *c.*1793–1820. Standard printed mark on stone china ware *c.*1805–20. Overglaze printed mark on porcelains *c.*1815–30. Standard printed mark *c.*1870–87.

Derby Porcelain from 1749. Bone china from 1805. Early Duesbury-Derby incised mark *c.*1750–55. Incised initial *c.*1770–80. Painted crown and 'D' usually blue, *c.*1770–82. Painted mock-Dresden mark *c.*1785–1825. Bloor Derby: painted or printed Bloor Derby marks *c.*1825–48.

Doulton Stoneware and earthenware, also porcelains at Burslem. Doulton Lambeth: standard impressed mark *c.*1820–54. Oval impressed mark *c.*1854–70. Impressed or printed mark on earthenware *c.*1872. Standard impressed mark *c.*1880–1902.

Herculaneum Liverpool pottery. High-grade earthenware and porcelain *c.*1793–1841. Early impressed name mark, very rare *c.*1793–1820. Full name mark normally impressed *c.*1822–33.

Heron Printed mark incorporating initials R.H. & S. *c.*1850–1929. Wemyss or Wemyss ware printed mark *c.*1920–29.

Liverpool Earthenware, tin enamelled earthenware from *c.*1710, cream-coloured earthenware *c.*1780, soft-paste porcelain rare, soapstone porcelain *c.*1756 'Chaffers' Liverpool. From *c.*1765 'Christian' Liverpool with high quality enamel decoration.

Longton Hall Rare painted mark in underglaze blue. *c.*1749–60.

Lowestoft Soft paste similar to Bow. Copies of blue Worcester crescent mark and Dresden crossed swords *c.*1775–90.

Mason 'patent ironstone china' Standard printed mark from *c.*1815. From *c.*1861 G.L. Ashworth & Bros. 1968 retitled 'Mason's Patent Ironstone China Ltd'.

Minton Porcelain and earthenware from 1793 to present day. Painted mark *c.*1805–16. Dresden crossed swords on floral encrusted wares 1820s. Various marks incorporating initials 'M' and 'M & B'. Standard printed mark *c.*1863–72. Revised *c.*1873.

New Hall Hard-paste type porcelain *c.*1781–1812. From 1812 standard bone china. Early porcelains without factory mark but boldly painted pattern number on hollow ware. Mainly tea ware produced.

Pinxton 1796–1813. Mainly unmarked, resembles Derby. Occasionally painted crescent and star mark. Porcelains.

Plymouth Hard-paste porcelain by William Cookworthy *c.*1768–70. Standard but rare chemical formula mark for tin painted underglaze or overglaze *c.*1768–70.

Rockingham Printed, impressed and moulded marks incorporating initial 'B' or 'Brameld' 1806–42. Printed griffin mark in red *c.*1826–30. Fine porcelain.

Swansea Pottery and fine porcelain *c.*1814–22. Three early impressed or painted marks on earthenwares. Basic name-mark printed overglaze or painted *c.*1814–22.

Wedgwood Earthenwares and porcelain. Basic impressed name mark from *c.*1759 (Josiah Wedgwood). Printed name mark on rare porcelains *c.*1812–22. Impressed mark with 'Etruria' *c.*1840–45. From 1860 impressed year letters.

Wedgwood & Co Earthenwares from *c.*1860–1965. Should not be confused with Josiah whose mark was simply 'Wedgwood' and not 'Wedgwood & Co (Ltd).'

Worcester Soft-paste porcelain and soapstone porcelain. This mark is too complicated to deal with in full here. Blue crescent *c.*1755–83, pseudo-Oriental and 'Dresden crossed swords' among First Period or 'Dr. Wall' period. Flight period 1783–92. Small crescent mark, and other marks incorporating name. Barr, also Flight & Barr Period 1792–1807. Standard incised 'B' often with small cross among several marks. Barr, Flight & Barr Period *c.*1807–13. Standard impressed or incised 'B.F.B.' marks with or without crown. Flight, Barr & Barr Period 1813–40. Standard impressed mark 'F.B.B.' under crown. Chamberlain's 1840–52. Standard impressed or printed mark without crown. Royal Worcester *c.*1862 to present day.

A collection of Royal Crown Derby miniatures in the Imari style. All *c.*1920. Prices from £60–100 for teapot to £400–600 for iron and stand.

Early 18th-century slipware porringer with yellow ground and brown decoration. 5⅜ in / 13.5 cm.
£2000–3000.

An 18th-century slipware candlestick in creamy yellow glaze with brown decoration. 3 in / 7.5 cm.
£3000–4000.

An 18th-century slipware puzzle jug decorated with sgraffito birds in yellow on deep-brown ground.
5½ in / 14 cm high.
£1500–2500.

Lambeth delft bleeding bowl with blue and manganese splash decoration *c.*1680. £4000–6000.

Late 17th-century English delft 'blue dash' charger with lead-glazed back, decorated in green, blue, orange and yellow. 13⅜in / 34cm diameter. £1500–2500.

English delft wet drug jar of globular shape painted in blue with putti and flowers, labelled 'Ol: Viride'. 7½in/ 19cm. £400–550.

An English delft dry drug jar painted in blue with birds, fruit and flowers, labelled 'U:Pomatum'. 6⅛in / 15.5cm. Early 18th century. £400–550.

Brislington delft portrait charger of William III decorated in blue, manganese and yellow. 13 in / 33 cm diameter. £5000–7000.

Brislington delft portrait charger, possibly of the Duke of Monmouth decorated in blue, manganese and yellow. 13⅛ in / 33.5 cm. £5000–7000.

Liverpool delft bowl with 'Fazakerley' style decoration in yellow, blue and manganese with green leaves. 9⅞ in / 25 cm diameter *c.* 1750. £700–1000.

Delft 'blue and white'

English delft tea caddy with blue and white 'chinoiserie' decoration of flowers and foliage with birds, and Jacob and Rebecca at the Well. 3⅞in / 9.7 cm. *c.*1720. £1500–2000.

Left English delft dish with everted rim decorated in blue and white with a Chinese scene. 13¾in / 35 cm diameter. Early 18th century. £300–500.

Right English or Dutch delft dish *c.*1700 decorated with a fox and goose chase, painted in blue with 'sponged' trees. £1000–1500.

London delft plate of Admiral Keppel with iron red rim and manganese inscription, the portrait in blue and white style. 8⅞in / 22.7 cm diameter. £500–700.

Lowestoft butter pot in moulded salt-glaze with fluted body and lid, and red borders. £210–280.

Staffordshire salt-glaze teapot with crabstock handle and enamelled decoration of a white rose and thistle with portrait of Charles Edward Stuart, probably later decoration. *c.* 1750. 5½ in / 14 cm high. £400–500.

Rare early teapot painted in polychrome colours of red, blue, green and yellow. 5⅜ in / 13.5 cm. £700–850.

Salt-glazed stoneware

Staffordshire white salt-glazed jar and cover formed as a bear with details in brown slip, second quarter of the 18th century. 8½ in / 21.5 cm high. £6000–7500.

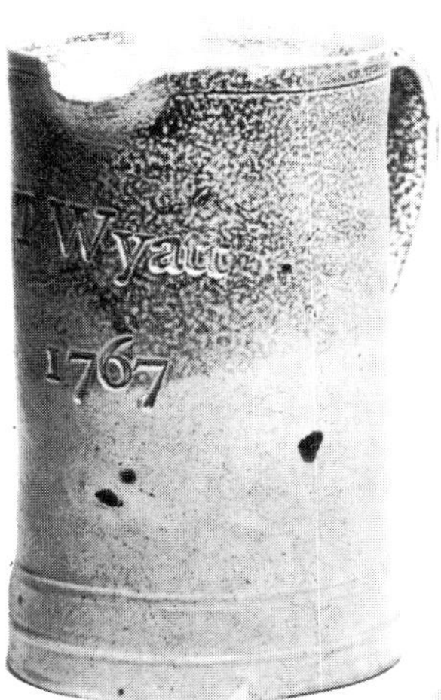

English brown stoneware jug, probably London, dated 1767. £300–500.

German 17th century salt-glazed bellarmine with stamped relief decoration of medallions on body and with bearded mask on neck. 14⅛ in / 36 cm. £300–400.

Whieldon teapot of globular shape with moulded fruiting vine decoration and crabstock handle, streaked with green, grey and manganese glaze *c.*1760. 4⅜in / 11 cm high. £1000–1300.

Wedgwood / Whieldon melon-shaped teapot with applied moulded leaf and flower decoration with leaf and stem handle, engine-turned with dots in 'egg and spinach' colours *c.*1760–65. £2500–3500.

Left Christian Liverpool teapot with strap handle and moulded fluted body decorated with scroll-edged panels with red scroll border. 6⅞in/17.5cm *c.*1765. £400–600.

Centre Worcester teapot with Chinese decoration of figures in panels outlined in puce with gilt scrolls. First period *c.*1765. 5¾in/14.5cm. £700–1000.

Right Lowestoft teapot of globular shape painted in green enamel outlined in black. Cypher mark 'AA'. 6½in/16.5cm. £600–800.

Worcester teapot of fluted barrel shape with flower finial, with deep blue border. First period crescent mark *c.*1775. 5⅜in/13.5cm. £1200–1400.

Worcester teapot of round globular shape with flower finial decorated with butterflies and birds in panels edged with gold rococo scrolls, with blue scale ground. First period *c.*1765–68. 5⅞in / 15cm. £1300–1800.

Above left Worcester barrel-shaped teapot with flower finial with sprays of flowers in panels edged with gold scrolls, on apple green ground. *c.*1770. 5½in/14cm high. £1500–2500. *Above right* Round globular-shaped teapot with flower finial decorated with garlands and insects, with flower finial and pale turquoise ground. *c.*1775. 5⅞in/15cm high. £300–500.

Worcester teapot with 'hop trellis' pattern with fluted barrel-shaped body decorated with green garlands, gold scrolls and puce herringbone border. *c.*1770–75. 5⅛in/13cm high. £2000–3000.

Left Longton Hall coffee can decorated in underglaze blue with 'Folly' pattern *c.*1775. £1500–1800. *Right* Bow miniature teapot with underglaze blue decoration of trailing vines. *c.*1765. 3¾in/9.5cm high. £700–900.

Above Liverpool 'Chaffers' octagonal soup plate painted with a Chinese landscape. *c.*1757. £500–800.

Early Worcester jug with enamelled decoration of Chinese scene, with pear-shaped body and plain spout. *c.*1755. £1200–1400.

Worcester blue and white coffee can with 'prunus fence' pattern *c.*1756. £1000– 1200.

Lowestoft miniature tea service in blue and white decorated with Chinese river scenes. £900–1600.

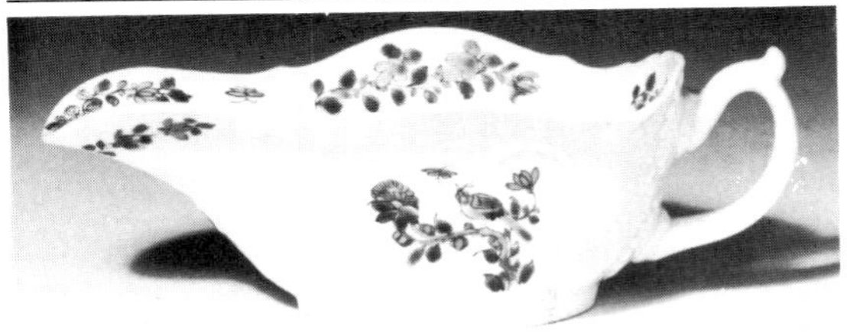

Early Worcester sauceboat of silver shape with moulded scroll decoration and 'famille rose' coloured enamels. *c.*1753–55. 6¼in/16cm. £1500–2200.

Worcester two-handled sauceboat with scallop moulded lip *c.*1756–58. 7⅜in/18.7cm. £600–800.

Worcester rococo sauceboat with raised wavy-edged sides. *c.*1755. 7⅝in/19.3cm. £600–800.

Early Worcester pickle dish in 'famille rose' coloured enamels and fluted shell shape. *c.*1753–55. 4⅝in/11.7cm. £800–1200.

Worcester sauceboat with 'famille rose' decoration in enamels with scroll handle *c.*1753. 6½in/16.5cm. £1500–2000.

Worcester sauceboat with gadroon moulding picked out in puce with puce scrollwork, painted in colours, with moulded fluted body. First period *c.*1760. 5⅞in/15cm. £600–800.

Chelsea plate moulded in rococo silver shape with panels of flowers painted in colours. Red anchor period 1752–56. 9in/23cm diameter. £1500–1800.

Chelsea peony flower dish with leaf and stem handle. Red anchor period 1752–56. 9 in/23 cm. £2000–2500.

Below Bow leaf sauceboat with puce ribbing to stem handle and green and yellow decoration. *c.*1760. £600–1000.

Above Chelsea cabbage-leaf bowl with green and yellow edging, painted in polychrome colours. Red anchor mark and period. 1752–56. 6¾ in/17 cm diameter. £2000–2500.

Chelsea acanthus moulded coffee cup and saucer with moulded leaf pattern and rococo handle. Red anchor period 1752–56. 3⅛ in/8 cm height. £800–1200.

Worcester coffee cup and saucer printed in lilac with classical landscape scenes with enamelled and gold decoration. First period *c.*1775. £500–650.

Left Liverpool creamware ship bowl inscribed 'Succefs to the Thomas and Sally' printed black outside with centre painted in colours *c.*1786. £1500–2000.

Above Rare Bow transfer-print plate with borders in grey-black and centre in lilac with 'St. George' and 'For our Country' probably by Robert Hancock. 9 in/23 cm diameter. *c.*1755. £1000–1500.

Worcester tankard printed in black by Robert Hancock with half-length portrait of William Pitt flanked by 'Fame' and 'Minerva'. *c.*1761. 5¾ in/14.7 cm. £1700–2200.

Staffordshire pearlware printed and coloured two-piece warmer, the base printed in black, washed with Pratt-type colours. *c.*1815. 9 in / 23 cm overall. £600–800.

Lowestoft jug with flat ball finial and spur handle printed and washed in heavy underglaze blue with some running of colour in the border, of early willow-type landscape. £500–700.

Above Part of a late 18th-century/early 19th-century willow pattern service in transfer-printed blue and white, probably Leeds. Plate £30–40, tureen £300–400, dish £100–150, sauce boat £75–100.

A collection of transfer-printed ware. *Left to right:* London to Birmingham train mug, sepia printed *c.*1887. Liverpool & Manchester railway lilac printed mug *c.*1830, Plate with black printed 'Hero' steam engine, brown printed train mug and a train mug printed black with enamel green and puce painting by Deakin. £100–200 each.

Chelsea octagonal tea bowls decorated with flower sprigs. Red anchor mark and period 1753–56. 2⅜in and 2¾in / 6cm and 7cm height. £500–700.

Chelsea bell-shaped coffee cup and 'trembleuse' saucer. Red anchor mark 1753–56. £600–800.

Longton Hall octagonal tea bowl and saucer painted in imitation Chelsea style. Middle period 1749–60. £650–850.

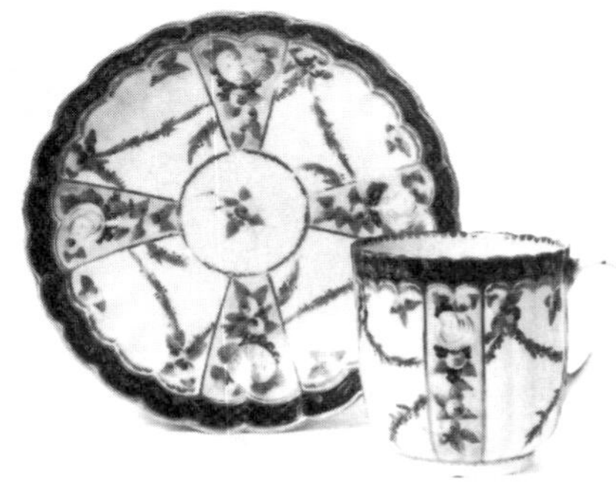

Worcester coffee cup and saucer of fluted form with deep blue border and four gilt diaper bands, on turquoise ground. First period 'W' in blue. *c.*1770. £1200–1500.

Chelsea tea bowl and 'trembleuse' saucer painted with sprays of flowers. Red anchor period 1752–56. £500–700.

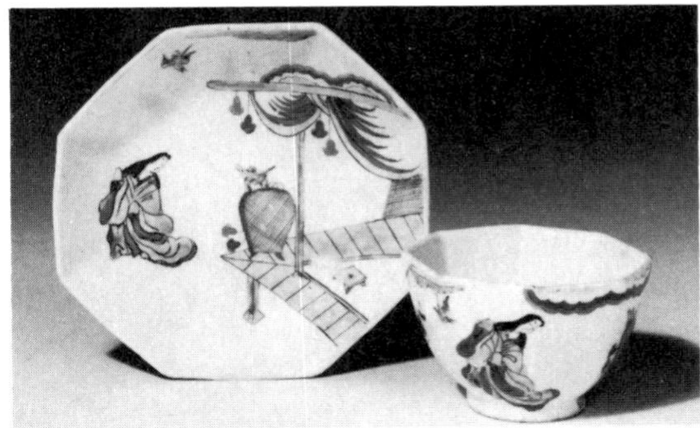

Chelsea octagonal tea bowl decorated in green, red and blue enamels with the 'lady and pavilion' Kakiemon pattern. Raised anchor period *c.*1750. £1500–2500.

Right Worcester tea bowl decorated in finely pencilled black. First period *c.*1755–83. £800–950.

Far right Chelsea tea bowl and saucer finely painted with birds and butterflies with a ladybird painted on the interior of the bowl. Red anchor mark 1753–56. £600–800.

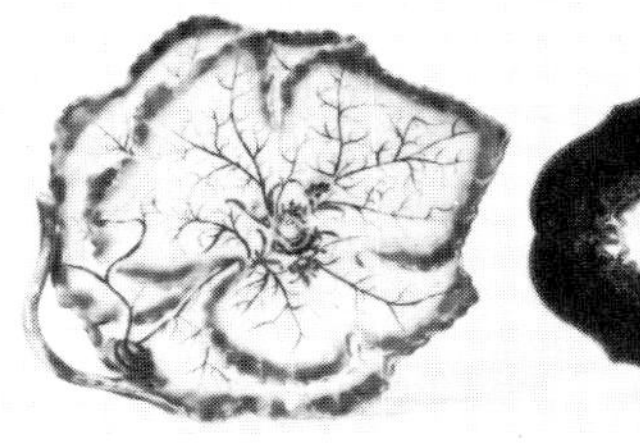

Worcester leaf dish with twig handle in brown and yellow, black veining on leaf and small moulded snail. Pierced for hanging. First period *c.*1760. 9 in / 23 cm. £900–1200.

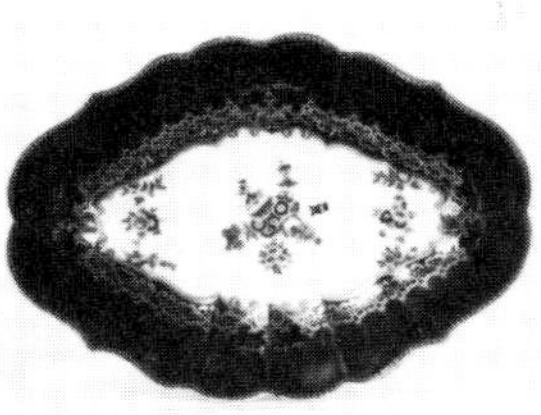

Worcester dessert dish of lobed oval shape, with deep wet-blue ground and gilt and enamel decoration. First period *c.*1770. 9⅜ in / 24 cm. £350–500.

Worcester lobed dessert dish with deep wet blue border and scalloped shape, decorated with garlands and an exotic bird. *c.*1775. £500–600.

Worcester scallop rimmed plate en suite. £350–500.

Right Worcester plate with wavy edge decorated with two exotic birds on branches. *c.*1770. 8⅞ in / 22.5 cm. £600–800.

Embossed Chelsea plate after a Meissen pattern, decorated with painted butterflies, with the rim edged in brown. Red anchor mark 1752–56. 9⅜ in / 23.7 cm. £700–900.

Worcester dessert centre dish with osier moulded border, raised on foot, with decorated underside and centre painted with fabulous birds. First period *c.*1765–70. £1400–1600.

Longton Hall strawberry plate with crisply moulded rim and centre painted with fabulous birds. *c.*1755. 10⅞in/27.5cm. £1500–2500.

Swansea shell-shaped dessert dish decorated with trailing vines in brown and gold and painted in sepia monochrome inscribed 'Marino, a Casino belonging to the Earl of Charlemont' by William Weston Young. Impressed Swansea. 8¼in/21cm. £600–800.

Worcester fan-pattern dessert dish with Japan-style decoration with central gilt mons, half mons in blue, red, green and gold, with blue inner border. Pseudo character mark. First period. c.1765–70. 7½in/19cm. £600–800.

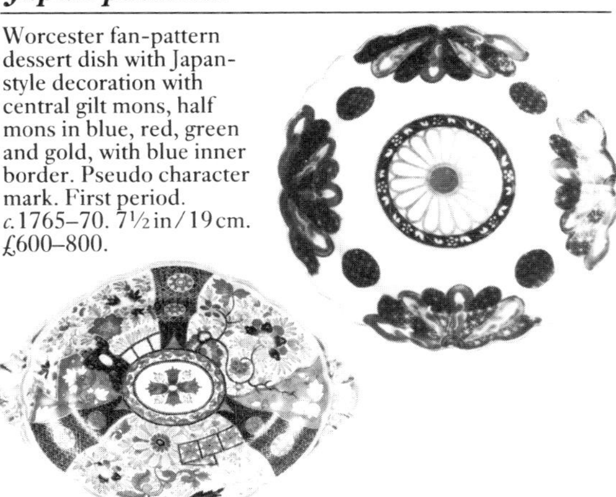

Worcester dessert dish decorated in red, blue, pink and green with deep blue divisions in the 'Japan' style. Flight & Barr period, incised 'B' mark. c.1805. £400–500.

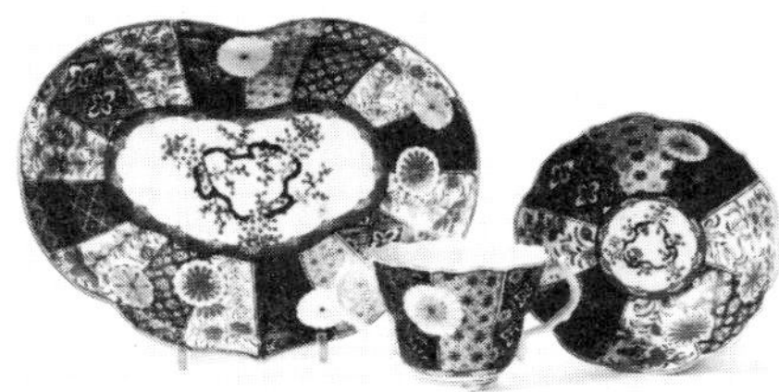

Left Worcester dessert dish with underglaze blue, painted in Japan colours, with pseudo Chinese marks. First period c.1770. £650–850. *Right* Worcester chocolate cup and saucer of ogee form with lamprey handles and 'Old Mosaic' pattern decorated in underglaze blue with 'Japan' colours. First period c.1770. £650–800.

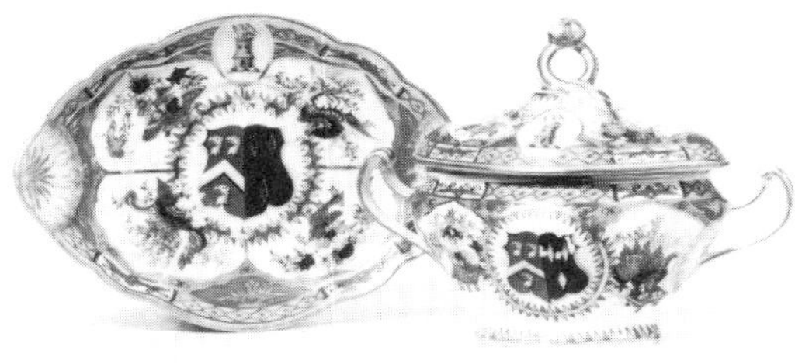

Chamberlain Worcester armorial sauce tureen, cover and stand decorated with the 'Kylin' pattern. 8¼in/21cm. c.1810. £800–1400.

Worcester moulded partridge tureens with chestnut brown decoration *c.*1756–58. 6⅛in/15.5cm. Pair: £1500–3000.

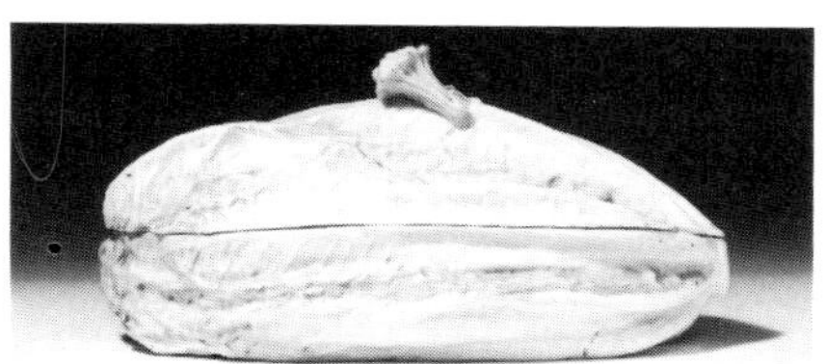

Longton Hall cos lettuce tureen with leaves edged in lettuce green and interior painted with leaves and flowers to hide kiln imperfections. Sprouting bud finial. *c.*1775. £2000–2500.

Derby chestnut basket with honeycomb moulded body and pierced lid and dish with applied twig and leaf handles, painted in blue with cruciform flowers and Chinese river landscapes. 8in/20cm across. £900–1200.

Derby chestnut basket with rope-twist finial, trellis-moulded body and cover, with pierced cover and applied flower decoration, painted with moths and cherries. Basket 8½in/21.5cm, dish 8¼in/21cm diameter. £400–600.

Liverpool 'Chaffers' creamware mug with strap handle and bell-shaped body, decorated with a dove and olive branch. *c.*1760. £2000–3000.

Bow tankard of bell shape with curved strap handle painted in colours with garlands and flowers and a ladybird, the inside rim decorated with puce spirals. *c.*1755–60. 3¼in/9.5cm. £600–800.

Worcester cylindrical tankard with deep blue scale ground, gold rococo scrolls and fabulous birds painted in colours. First period *c.*1770. 5⅞in/15cm. £1200–1500.

Pinxton porter mug, engine-turned with chequer pattern, and a border of pink roses on a black ground with gold bands. Late 18th century. 5⅜in/13.5cm. £120–280.

New Hall presentation jug decorated with peonies and roses, a gilt Greek key neckband and a gilt monogram 'TG'. *c.*1785. 7½ in/19 cm. £700–1200.

Above Worcester blue-scale cabbage-leaf jug with mask spout and ring handle decorated with scrolling rococo gold-outlined panels with flowers. 5⅞ in/23 cm. *c.*1770. £1000–1500.

Above left Worcester cabbage-leaf mask jug with ring handle and printed decoration of flowers and trailing vines. First period *c.*1765. 9 in/23 cm. £400–600.
Above right Early New Hall type jug with moulded overlapping cabbage leaves with puce leaf and red star motifs, edged with blue enamel. 5½ in/14 cm. *c.*1790. £250–350.

Right Bristol hard-paste jug with mask spout, painted in colours with sprigs of flowers. £400–600.

New Hall bone china tea and coffee set with coffee cans and tea cups printed with fruit, with gilded rims. *c.*1815. £1400–1700 (45 pieces).

A New Hall style tea set decorated in yellow and gold with 12 tea bowls and coffee cups, in hybrid hard-paste porcelain. *c.*1790. £800–1200.

Caughley tea service with vertical flutes, decorated by Chamberlain of Worcester in gilt with blue enamel berries. £1800–2100.

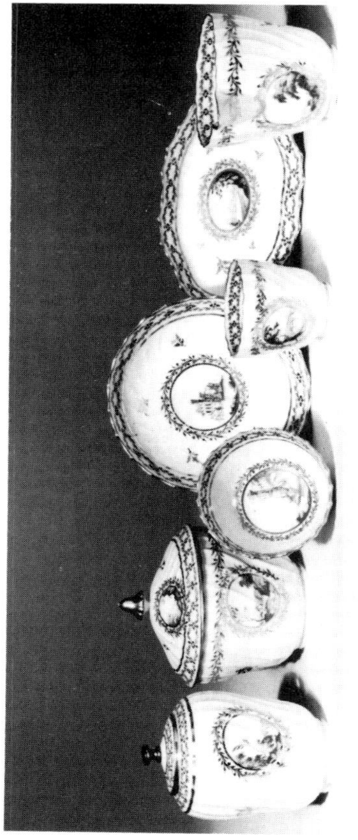

Caughley 'shanked' tea service painted with landscapes, different on each piece, surrounded with gold wreaths and polychrome leaves. *c.*1790. £3000–4000.

Derby tea service in 'Smith's blue' with gilt cartouche, painted with landscapes surrounded with blue enamel bands. *c.*1785. £2700–3500 (45 pieces).

Spode tea set decorated with cabbage rose pattern no. 2812. *c.*1815. £1200–1500 (45 pieces).

Spode tea set decorated with a 'Japan' pattern border. *c.*1815. £1800–2400 (45 pieces).

Belleek 'spiders' web' tea set wtih twig handles and scalloped rims, with two cups and saucers. Late 19th century. £1000–1500.

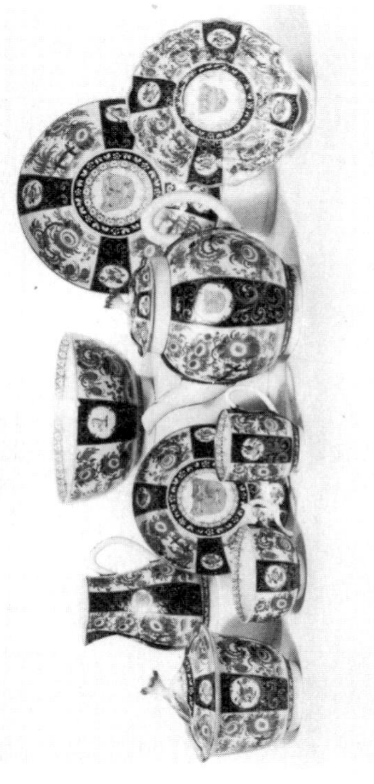

Worcester armorial tea service with flower finials, decorated in 'Kakiemon' Japan coloured enamels. *c.*1770. £10 000–15 000 (45 pieces including twelve 'trios').

Spode dessert service derived from silver shapes, painted in 'Japan' colours. *c.*1815. £1500–2000 (27 pieces).

Below Pearlware dessert service boldly painted with ornithological pattern with gilt line borders. £900–1500 (31 pieces).

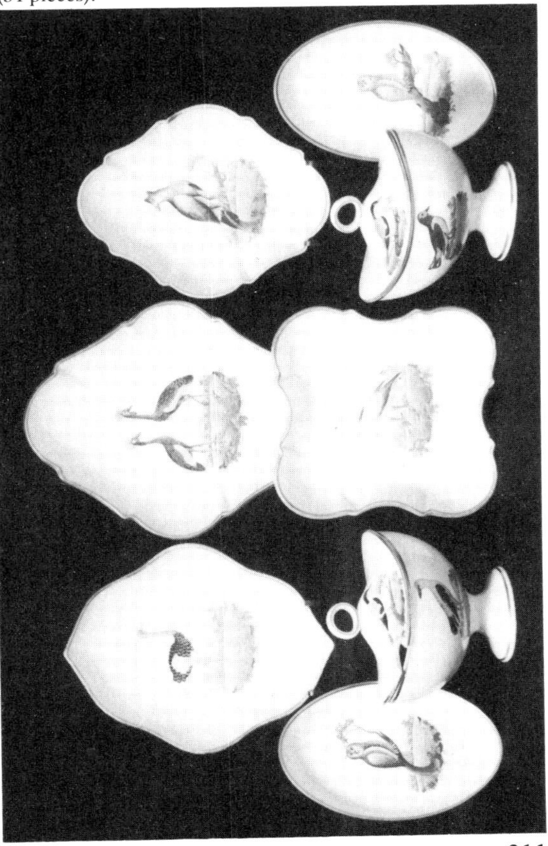

Caughley dessert service in underglaze blue with a formal flower pattern and gilded borders, in lobed and fluted shapes. 45 pieces including a pair of ice pails. *c.*1790. £3000–4000.

Derby dessert service with lime green borders and formal gilded borders, painted with landscapes. 36 pieces including pairs of tureens and ice pails. *c.*1800. £6000–8000.

Coalport dessert service with deep blue borders and rococo gilded scrollwork painted with wild birds with gilt beaded borders. Mock Sèvres marks enclosing 'R'. £800–1000.

Davenport dessert service with pink borders and gilded scrollwork, painted with landscapes, with printed marks 'Davenport, Longport, Staffordshire'. £2000–3000 (18 pieces).

Rare Wedgwood bone china dessert service with a matt jet black ground and puce leaves. Marked 'Wedgwood' in red. Pattern no. 686. *c.*1815. £2500–3500 (32 pieces).

J. & W. Ridgway ironstone dessert service with dark blue ground and gilt diaper, painted with landscapes surrounded by 'salmon scale' border with scrolling leaf and flower handles. *c.*1835. £3500–4500 (38 pieces).

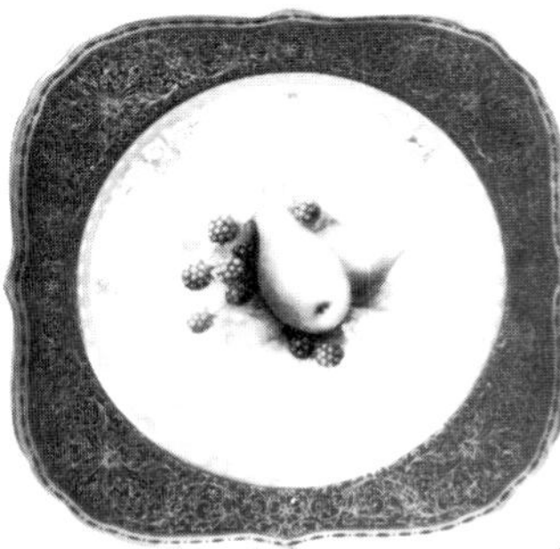

Royal Worcester dessert plate with claret ground borders finely decorated with gilt tracery and gilt borders. Signed A. Shuck. 1925. £150–200.

Royal Worcester dessert plate with deep blue borders decorated with gilt rococo husks, swags and scrolls, the centres filled with fruit. Signed R. Sebright. 1926. 9 in / 23 cm diameter. £350–450.

Left Royal Worcester dessert plate by Richard Sebright with deep blue and pale pink panelled grounds with raised gold and scroll border. 1917. 8⅝ in / 22 cm diameter. £250–300.

Royal Worcester dessert plate with deep blue ground and gold sprays, painted with landscape by G. Johnson. Date code for 1909. £160–230.

Rockingham miniature teapot in the Dresden manner with applied flowers, decorated in gilt with green twig handle. Griffin mark in red. 2½ in / 6.5 cm. *c.*1828–30. £350–500.

Cabinet cup and stand, possibly Welsh, with 'biting snake' handle, a pale primrose yellow ground with wide gold border band, of similar shape to Swansea. *c.*1818. £300–500.

Ecuelle and cover flanked by two cups and stands with handles of 'eagle and lamprey in combat', decorated with bands of simulated pearls, bordered with white and gilt with seaweed pattern. Barr Flight & Barr. 7¾ in / 19.5 cm. *c.*1810. Cups £500–700 each. Ecuelle £800–1400.

Spode spill vases in bright 'Japan' colours with beaded rims, marked in red SPODE 967. 6¼in and 4⅜in / 16 cm and 11 cm. *c.*1820. £1000–1500.

Minton 'pate-sur-pate' vases with decoration of elves and fairies on a deep slate-blue ground and gilt borders with 'Dog of Fo' handles. 1890. 16⅛in / 41 cm. £4000–5000 pair.

Bloor Derby garniture of classical urn shape with scrolling leaf-capped handles with dark blue ground and gilt decoration. 11¼in and 8⅞in / 28.5 cm and 22.5 cm. *c.*1830. £1300–1600.

Royal Worcester garniture with pierced necks and scroll feet in bronze and gold, painted with Highland cattle by Harry Stinton. Date code for 1911. £1700–2000.

Pair of Minton candlesticks of pedlar boy and flower girl, with applied flowers in 'Dresden' manner, painted in colours and gilded. 8⅞in/22.5cm. *c.*1830–35. £1200–1500.

A pair of Coalbrookdale candlesticks edged in green and gilt with painted flower panels with applied flowerheads on rococo bases. 9⅝in/24.5cm. *c.*1830. £800–1200.

Minton table centrepiece with heavily gilt dolphin columns supporting three shells on the lower tier applied with flowers, with basket of coloured flowers above. *c.*1830–35. £1000–1400.

Minton bowl with scrolled gilt feet heaped with flower heads and berries, in full relief. Pseudo Meissen crossed swords mark. $10\frac{5}{8}$in / 27cm. *c.*1830. £1500–2000.

Wedgwood black basalt two-handled vase with classical decoration in red encaustic technique, known as 'antique vases of black porcelain'. Impressed Wedgwood. *c.*1790. £1200–1600.

Above Wedgwood jug in black basalt with relief frieze of putti and trees, and a silver-mounted rim. Impressed Wedgwood. *c.*1800. £400–600.

Wedgwood black basalt two-handled vase with classical decoration in red encaustic technique. Late 18th century. Impressed Wedgwood. £1000–1300.

Wedgwood cabinet coffee can and saucer in 'Trophy' pattern with black jasper dip ground and applied decoration in white, of rams' heads, swags and garlands. Impressed Wedgwood. Early 19th century. £500–700.

Wedgwood three-colour jasper coffee can and saucer of mosaic-type pattern with vertical flower and leaf bands. Early 19th century. £600–800.

Wedgwood blue jasper dip teapot with scenes of 'Domestic Employment' in white relief, with fluted base. Impressed Wedgwood. 4¾in/12cm. Late 18th century. £700–1000.

Above Green jasper dip cream jug with acanthus lip and putti in white relief with fluted base. Impressed Wedgwood. $2\frac{7}{8}$in / 7.5 cm. *c.*1820. £250–350.

Wedgwood green jasper dip Portland vase with loop handles with bearded mask terminals and decoration in applied white relief, with a classical half-length portrait on the base. Impressed Wedgwood. $10\frac{5}{8}$in / 27 cm high. Early 19th century. £1000–2000.

Wedgwood blue jasper dip butter dish with putti and acanthus leaves in white relief. Impressed Wedgwood in lower case mark. $6\frac{5}{8}$in / 17 cm diameter. *c.*1785. £600–800.

Above Circular bowl with 'fairyland' pattern in blue and gold bordered panels with base shaded in purple and blue, the interior decorated with poplar trees. 8¼ in / 21 cm diameter. £550–650.

Vase bordered with fish on a light green ground with 'Firbolgs' and 'Thumbelina' fairies in black and gold on claret ground. 8⅞ in / 22.5 cm diameter. £600–800.

Octagonal bowl with 'fairyland' pattern in blue and gold bordered panels with base shaded in purple and blue, decorated with woodland scenes, the interior with elves and fairies. 8⅞ in / 22.5 cm diameter. £800–900.

Doulton Lambeth oviform vases decorated by Eliza Banks in white, brown and green with 'pate-sur-pate' technique. 1883. 12¼in/315cm. £350–450.

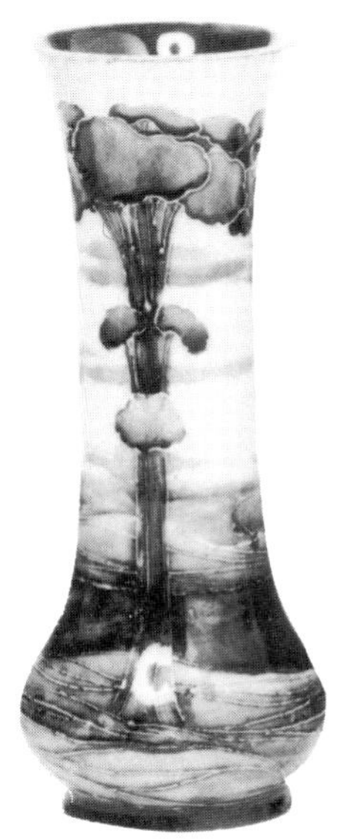

Examples of Moorcroft pottery with typical tube-line decoration. *Left* A 'Hazeldene' vase. 5in/17½cm. £200–300. *Right* A Moorcroft Macintyre vase. £200–300.

Above Selection of Wemyss pottery. *Left* Pig with shamrock, marked Wemyss. 17 in / 50 cm. £4000–6000. *Right* pig marked 'Wemyss Made in England'. £3500–4500. *Above* Duck flower holder. £500–800.

Right Royal Worcester vase and cover, painted with fruit, signed Ricketts. Date code for 1925. 10 in / 25.5 cm. £1000–1250.

Left Moorcroft Macintyre 'Florian ware' vase of double gourd shape with olive-coloured leaves on a white ground. 6⅞ in / 17.5 cm. £350–500.

Royal Worcester ewer, painted with swans in flight, with gilt acanthus leaf moulding and high scrolled leaf-capped handle. Signed C. Baldwyn. Shape no. 1309. Date code for 1907. 15⅜in / 39cm. £2500–3500.

Royal Worcester pot pourri vase and cover, painted with sheep in a landscape with simulated basket-weave base and pierced cover. Signed H. Davis. Date code for 1925. 11⅞in / 30cm. £1800–2200.

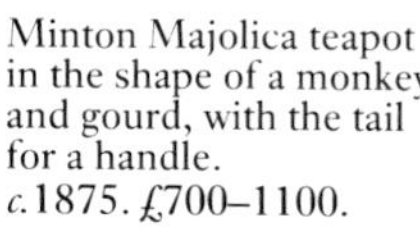

Minton Majolica teapot in the shape of a monkey and gourd, with the tail for a handle.
*c.*1875. £700–1100.

Martinware grotesque jug in the shape of a bird with blue and green wings. Incised mark dated 1906.
£5000–7000.

Right Staffordshire 'flatback' group 'Auld Lang Syne'. £130–150.

Right & below Royal Worcester candle extinguishers. 1880–1900. Owl £100–150. Jenny Lind (singer known as the 'Swedish nightingale') £200–300. Monk £80–100.

Above & above right Doulton stonewares decorated with animal subjects by Hannah Barlow. 1874–1903. Vase 12 in/31.5 cm. £400–600. *Left* £200–500.
Right Royal Doulton whisky flask in 'Kingsware' made for Dewar's Scotch Whisky. Churchwarden pattern. 9 in/24.5 cm. Early 20th century. £300–400.
Below John Barleycorn character jug modelled by C. J. Noke 1934. Rare factory mark. £200–300.

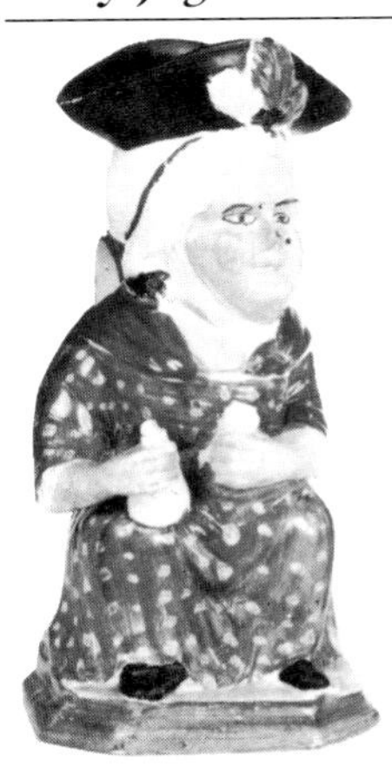

'Martha Gunn' Brighton bathing woman with gin bottle and Prince of Wales feathers in her hat. 10¼in/26cm. £800–1200.

Lord Rodney, possibly by Ralph Wood Jnr., related to the Derby series of admirals by Stephan. 12½in/32cm. £800–1200.

Right Toby jug possibly by Ralph Wood Jnr. Staffordshire, with pale blue coat and puce breeches 10⅜in/26.3cm. £450–550.

Below Ralph Wood Toby jug with olive coat and green waistcoat. *c.*1780. 10in/25.3cm. £1000–1500.

Below Toby jug of Ralph Wood type with light brown coat and yellow breeches. 10⅛in/25.8cm. £500–750.

Whieldon type lion splashed and sponged in manganese, cobalt and ochre on a green base. 3⅛in / 8cm high. *c.*1770. £400–500.

Whieldon type lion splashed only in manganese. 2¾in / 7cm. Late 18th century. £300–350.

Staffordshire lion with ochre spots and manganese mane. 2¾in / 7cm. Pratt type. *c.*1790. £120–150.

Staffordshire lamb on modelled base, sponged with orange. 2¾in / 7cm. *c.*1800. £140–170.

Staffordshire lamb sponged with orange and black. 2⅜in / 6cm. £50–80.

Above Wedgwood service of Travel pattern, designed by Eric Ravilious, printed in black and light blue. Early 1950s. Price range £15–20 small jug; £30–50 large dish.

Above Group of 20th century studio pottery. Leaping salmon vase by Bernard Leach. £500–700. Beaker by Bernard Leach. £150–250. Bowl by Charles Vyse. £150–200. Dish by Michael Cardew. £150–200. Vase by Michael Cardew. £80–100.

Right Pilkington 'Royal Lancastrian' vase by Gordon Forsyth. 1908. £350–450.

Yorkshire pottery two-storey moneybox with male and female standing figures, blue roof, orange and green decoration and children at the upper windows. 4½in/11.5cm. Early 19th century. £250–400.

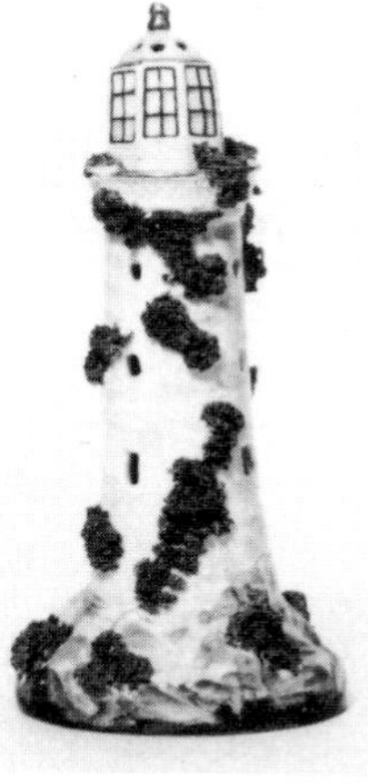

Lighthouse encrusted with moss with pierced slit windows. *c.*1840. £300–500.

Above Octagonal pavilion encrusted with vegetation with pierced slits. 3⅜in/8.5cm. £175–220.

Staffordshire pottery pastille burner with green vegetation. 3½in/9cm. *c.*1830. £200–300.

Pastille burners

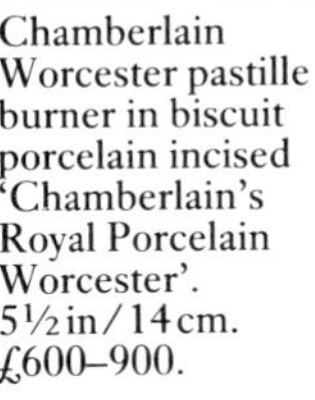

Chamberlain Worcester pastille burner in biscuit porcelain incised 'Chamberlain's Royal Porcelain Worcester'. 5½ in/14 cm. £600–900.

Left Pastille burner with Gothic windows on separate base. 5½ in/14 cm. *c.* 1835. £150–200.

Pastille burner of Gothic folly with columns and twisting chimney. 5⅝ in/14.5 cm. *c.* 1835. £200–250.

Pastille burner with applied coloured flowers. 5½ in/14 cm. *c.* 1840. £150–200.

Above left Dish by Charlotte Rheed in Bursley ware. Signed. *c.*1930. £150–250. *Right* Shallow bowl with Art Deco design by Clarice Cliff. Newport pottery mark. *c.*1930. £250–350.

Right Wedgwood plate painted by E. Lessore with moulded lobed border. Impressed Wedgwood. 9⅜in / 24cm. £50–70.

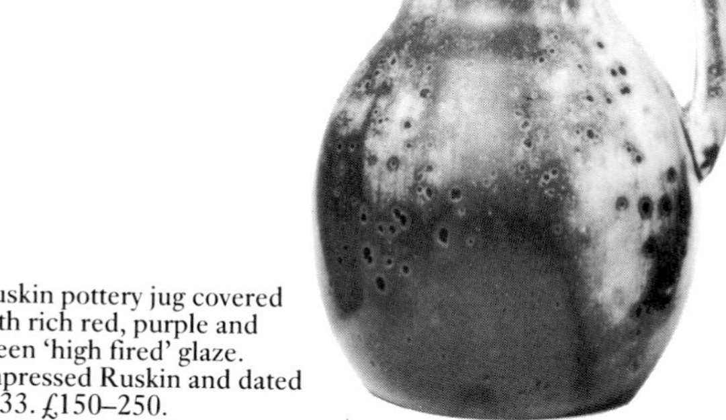

Ruskin pottery jug covered with rich red, purple and green 'high fired' glaze. Impressed Ruskin and dated 1933. £150–250.

Glass

In contrast to almost every other field of antique buying and collecting, the field of English glass has not kept pace with rapidly rising prices, and today it could be said that it is undervalued in comparison with other sections of the market. There are many explanations for this, but none of them are very satisfactory. In all probability glass remains the least-favoured field because people find it rather cold and impersonal, and it needs to be well displayed to be properly appreciated. There is also a general feeling that it is too breakable to use and enjoy, and too fragile to spend much money on. This is understandable but curious, because the amount of glass which has survived from the 18th century onwards should be proof enough that, on the contrary, it is remarkably tough and enduring.

On the other hand, a whole new field has opened up over the past few years in buying and collecting 19th- and even 20th-century glass, of a kind which for years has been dismissed as unimportant, bad taste, or just plain old-fashioned. The interest in glass as a decorative material was revived in the 19th century, with new and rediscovered processes and techniques of staining, colouring, overlaying and flashing, as well as reproducing the ancient and grand 'façon de Venise' glass of 16th-century Italy. These highly decorative pieces have attracted a following of new collectors who have little interest in the more purist, aesthetic appreciation of English 18th-century glass. Both are still relatively small collecting fields, and of the two it is 19th- and 20th-century glass which today commands the higher price.

English glass

The history of English glass begins in about 1670 when George Ravenscroft obtained a licence to produce a new formula glass called 'flint glass' or 'glass of lead'. Until then the monopoly for making and supplying glass to England had been held by the Venetians, whose glass was made to a different formula, seldom brilliantly clear and often with a pale straw-coloured or greenish tinge. Until his licence expired, only Ravenscroft's glass houses at Henley-on-Thames and in London produced his new formula glass, but as soon as they were able, glass houses all over England began to make 'glass of lead' to Ravenscroft's formula.

As with pottery and porcelain, glass-making depends on the availability of raw materials – basically a particularly vitreous white sand, calcined flint and potash – and the glass houses established themselves on sites where the sand existed naturally in the soil and there were plentiful stands of timber to fire the furnaces and provide the 'pearl ash' or potash made from calcined wood-ash which was a vital ingredient. While Ravenscroft's formula produced a glass described as 'crystal' because of its remarkable brilliance and clarity, it was not as easily workable as Venetian-type 'soda' glass which cooled slowly and could be worked into wonderful shapes. The original intention of English glass-makers had been simply to copy the shapes of Continental glass, but it was soon discovered that the new formula could not be worked in the same way. Thus evolved the plainer shapes of English drinking glasses, from the 'rummer' to early baluster glasses. The 'rummer' was derived from the 'roemer' an early bowl-shaped drinking glass for drinking popular Rhenish wine. The English 'roemer' had a heavy solid stem, unlike the Continental original which was basically a bowl flaring from a cylinder-shaped hollow base, decorated with strawberry prunts and glass thread. The solid-stemmed 'rummer' was soon adapted into a wide variety of bowl-shapes on baluster stems, and made in quantity by all the principal English glass houses, in Bristol, Stafford, Stourbridge, Newcastle, King's Lynn, Henley-on-Thames and London.

Fashion and function

From the capacity of early English drinking glasses such as the rummer, one can guess that wine was drunk 'by the bucket' as well as ale. At the beginning of the 18th century, fortified wines began to come into England from Portugal which required different treatment from clarets and Rhenish wines. Port, sherry and madeira needed decanters with airtight stoppers so that they would keep, and clear glass was required in order to show off their clear, sediment-free colours, as well as smaller glasses to drink them from. Wines were usually served from jugs and ewers filled from the barrel and were often cloudy.

Drinking is convivial, involving toasts, ceremonies and special occasions, and many glasses were engraved with commemorative motifs. English glass was a better medium for engraving than 'soda' glass, and quantities of it were exported, particularly to the Netherlands, for the same purpose. Most wine glasses were made with a conical folded foot during the first three decades of the 18th century. The conical shape lifted the uneven break of the 'pontil' clear of the surface, and the folded foot gave extra strength to the foot rim and was almost impossible to chip.

The 'pontil' was to be found on almost all glasses up to about 1750. It was not part of the finished glass itself, but was added to the blown but still molten piece when the mouth and rim were cut and smoothed, after which the glass was knocked off, leaving a mark where the pontil had been broken off. This slightly jagged mark in the centre of the base had been taken as an infallible guide to dating, but since it is remarkably simple to copy, it should not be taken as definitive proof of age. After about 1750 foot rims were no longer folded but ground flat and the pontil was generally ground off.

The pontil or 'punty' was reintroduced as a genuine part of glass manufacture in the 19th century when press-moulded glass was fire-polished – and incidentally, many reproductions of 18th-century glass were made.

Periods and styles

It was not fashion which proved the great stimulus to change in English glass, but a swingeing tax of 20 per cent on all clear glass imposed in 1745 which jolted the glassmakers into new methods of making drinking glasses. Before that date the baluster, light or heavy, was the rule, with fluted ale glasses, heavy-footed firing glasses and 'dram' glasses for the increasing consumption of spirits. In addition, 'deceptive' glasses were made for those who felt unequal to drinking a full measure for every toast and still remaining on their feet. There were cordial glasses for strong spirits and tavern 'cans' or mugs for beer and cider, decanters and claret jugs and a great variety of table ware. Decoration was limited to wheel engraving, stipple engraving and diamond engraving, and coloured glass was reserved for the lowly manufacture of wine bottles, dark green or brown. The imprisoned air bubble or teardrop was the only other embellishment, in stems and knops.

After 1745, enamelling took the place of engraving, for a certain amount of glass was wasted in the powder removed by the engraver, and the air bubble was converted into the air-twist stem, a purely English invention which lightened the weight. Coloured glass, exempt from tax, was used for table ware and drinking glasses. Opaque white twists, also tax exempt, were made from *c.*1755, colour twists from about the same period. From about 1760 facet-cut stems were introduced as another method of cutting the weight.

In 1776 the tax on glass was doubled, making it impossible for English glassmakers to continue producing the richer, heavier, cut glass which styles of the day demanded, and in 1780 many of the most famous names in English glassmaking fled to Ireland, which was granted free trade with England. Most of the highly-prized Irish glass, including Waterford, was made by one-time Stourbridge makers, using the same formulae and designs. The quality of the glass differed slightly and was heavier, richer and more brilliant because of the slight increase in lead content. Without the problems of tax to curb their production, Irish glass houses were profligate in cut glass of every kind, rich, heavy and lustrous. The English glass houses with continuing ingenuity resorted to splash enamel, trailed white glass over a coloured body typified by 'Nailsea' glass, and innumerable small novelty pieces made from 'cullet' the waste glass melted down and used again.

Nineteenth century glass

In 1825 Ireland imposed its own tax on glass, but by this time new techniques had been developed in America and on the Continent, and press-moulding, staining, colouring, flashing and casing were soon used in England to manufacture an entirely new range for the domestic market. Cut glass of heavy quality continued to be in great demand, but around 1830 the cutting became simpler, in plain flutes and horizontal bands, instead of the complex patterns of the beginning of the century. In 1845 the duty on glass was finally removed, and in the few years before the Great Exhibition of 1851 the English glass industry underwent a complete change, introducing a plethora of new techniques, both new and imported, from its new industrial base at Stourbridge.

Dates and sequence of baluster shapes

Inverted baluster	1682–1710
Drop knop	1690–1710
Angular knop	1695–1715
Ball knop	1695–1715
Annulated knop (triple ring)	1695–1725
Multiple knops	1700–1720
True baluster	1710–1730
Acorn knop	1710–1715
Silesian stem	1715–1730
Air-twists	from *c.*1745
Opaque white twists	from *c.*1755
Colour twists	from *c.*1755
Facet cut stems	from *c.*1760

Globe-and-shaft shaped wine bottle in olive green glass. *c.*1660. 8½in/21.5cm. £1200–1700.

Green glass plain wine bottle of mallet shape, mid- to late 18th century. £30–45.

Club-shaped decanter engraved with three-masted man o'war 'Victory' and on the reverse 'Orange Broker', *c.*1810. 12in/30.5cm. £700–1100.

Cut glass decanter with star-cut mushroom stopper, etched with stemmed flowers, from a travelling case *c.*1820. £180–250.

Irish decanters and bulls' eye stoppers by Waterloo Co. Cork, with triple-ringed collars, engraved with stars and swags, moulded marks, *c.*1800. Pair: £800–1200.

Cut glass water jug with hobnail panels, fine diamond horizontal slice-cut neck, early 19th century. 8 in / 20.3 cm. £250–350.

Right Victorian English 'rock crystal' jug or ewer with ovoid body engraved with cupids fishing and prunus flower decoration to the faceted neck, *c.*1870. 10½ in / 27 cm. £300–500.

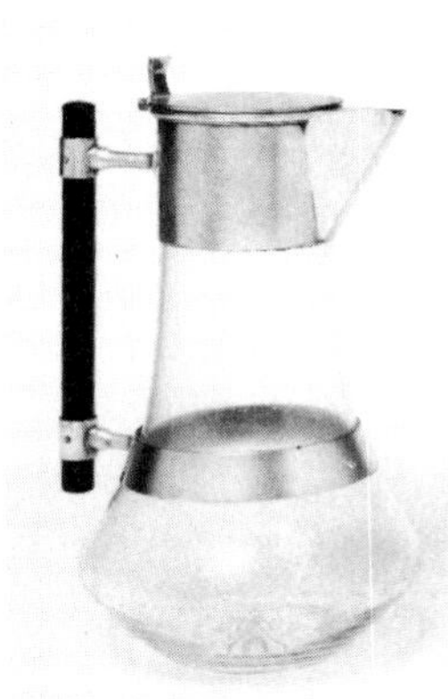

Glass claret jug with plated metal mounts with ebonised wood handle designed in the manner of Christopher Dresser. 9¼ in / 23.5 cm. £80–150.

Lemonade jug with plated metal mounts and moulded patterned foot, etched with 'Lemonade' and with ebonised wood handle, designed in the manner of Christopher Dresser. 9¼ in / 23.5 cm. £80–150.

Overlay glass goblet shaped vase in deep red overlaid in white and enamelled in colours, *c.*1860. 12¾in/32.5cm. English or Bohemian. £400–600.

Roemer-shaped goblet engraved with Bacchanalian scene of Silenus lying drunkenly beneath trailing vines, plain stem and cushion knop with tears, on a wide domed foot. Early 18th century. 10⅞ in / 27.5 cm. £600–1000.

Baluster goblet with round funnel bowl, cushioned mushroom knop with tear, knopped stem with tear and basal knop, on domed foot, *c.*1710–15. 7⅝ in / 19.5 cm. £900–1200.

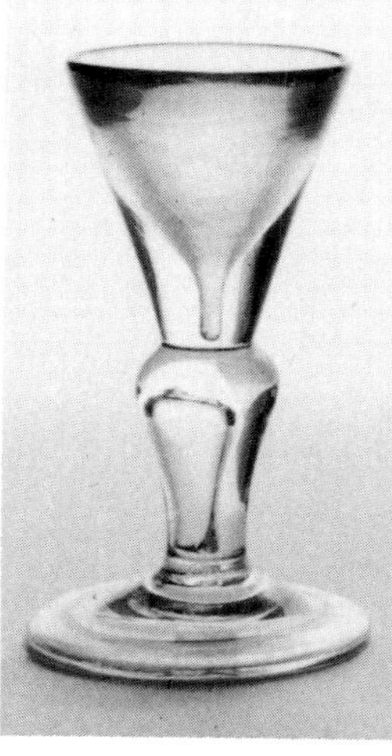

Toastmaster's wine glass with deceptive conical bowl and inverted baluster stem with tear in base, on folded conical foot, *c.*1720. 4¾in/12cm. £150–250.

Jacobite portrait firing glass with drawn trumpet bowl and heavy 'firing' foot, *c.*1750. 3¾in/9.5cm. £2500–3500.

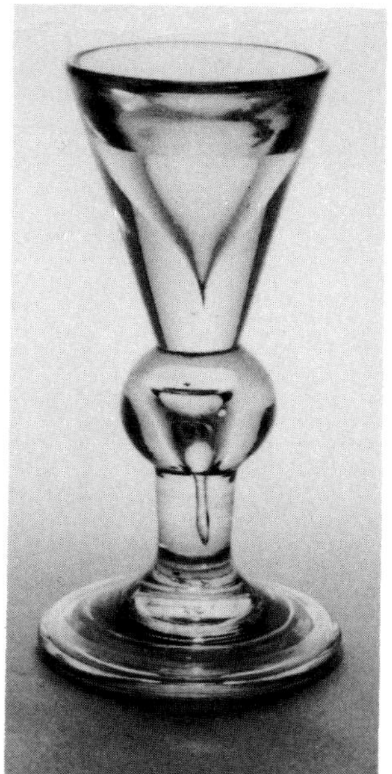

Deceptive glass with funnel bowl, ball knop, short stem with tear, on conical folded foot. *c.*1710–20. 5in/12.5cm. £180–300.

Baluster wine glass, with bell bowl on a double collar, fine baluster stem with tear, basal knop and folded foot. *c.* 1720. 6 in / 15.5 cm. £400–500.

Baluster wine glass with funnel bowl, three-ringed annulated knop and domed folded foot. 5½ in / 14 cm. £180–250.

A Dutch engraved wine glass engraved with armorials with two small cushion knops above an inverted baluster with a small tear, on wide conical foot engraved with the Royal Arms of England. 7½ in / 19 cm. £900–1200.

Baluster wine glass with bell bowl, three-ringed annulated knop and basal knop on folded conical foot, *c.*1720. 6 in/15 cm. £400–500.

Baluster wine glass with round funnel bowl, teared true and inverted baluster knops divided by a collar, on domed and folded foot, *c.*1715. 6 in/15.5 cm. £500–800.

Waisted bucket baluster wine glass with bowl with flattened knop, collar, and teared dumbell knop on folded spreading foot, *c.*1720. 5¼ in/13.5 cm. £400–600.

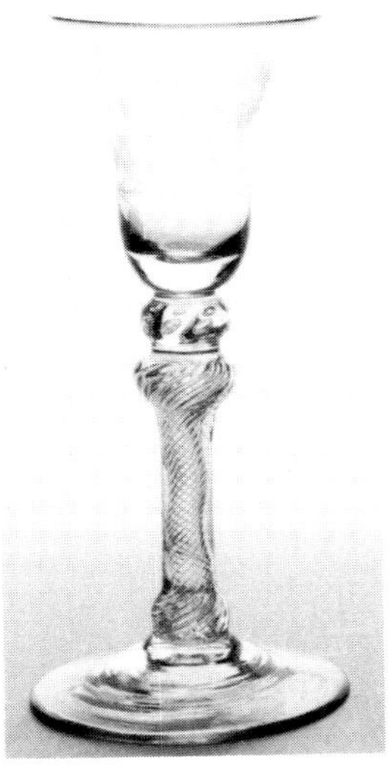

Wine glass with engraved bell bowl, teared and shoulder knops with multiple spiral air-twist stem on conical folded foot. *c.*1740–50. 6⅛in/15.7cm. £300–500.

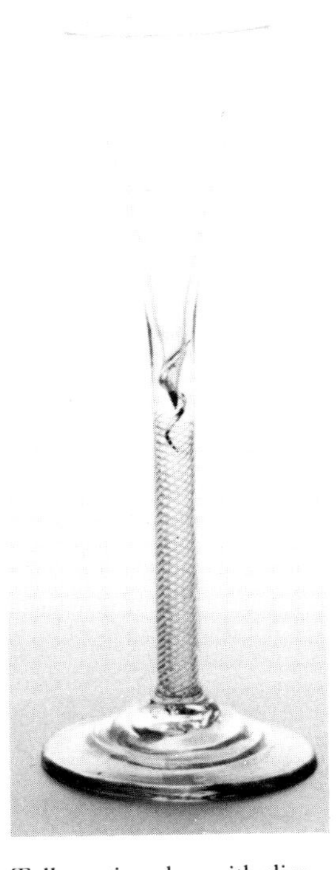

Tall toasting glass with slim drawn trumpet bowl and multiple spiral air-twist stem. *c.*1750. 7½in/19cm. £300–400.

Wine glass with round funnel bowl and loose spiral gauze opaque twist. 6in/15cm. £80–120.

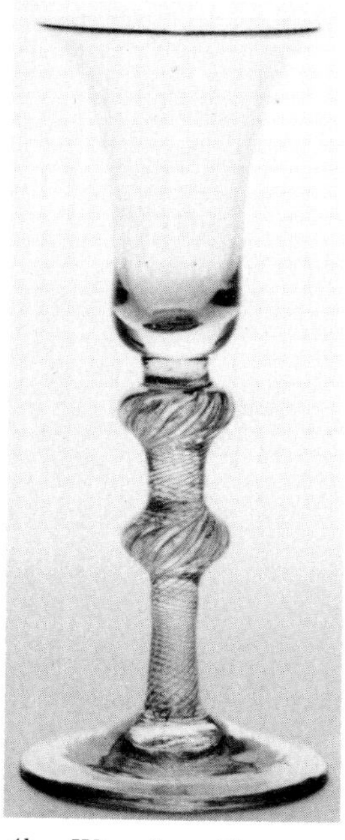

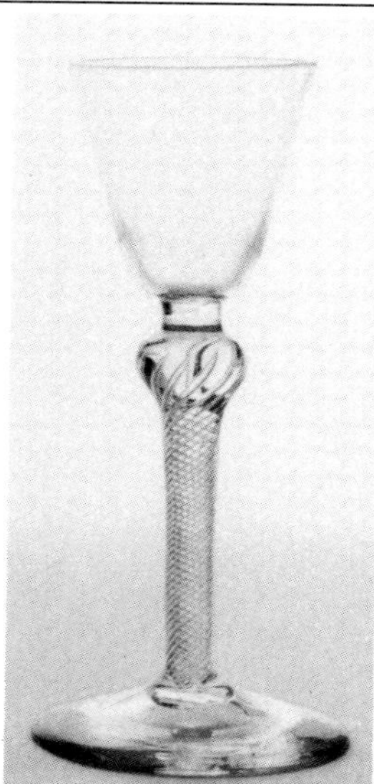

Above Wine glass with slender bell bowl, shoulder and centre knop and multiple spiral air-twist stem on conical folded foot, *c.*1750. 6½in/16.5cm. £150–200.

Above, right Wine glass with round funnel bowl, shoulder knop and multiple spiral air-twist stem on conical foot, *c.*1750. 6⅛in/15.7cm. £120–160.

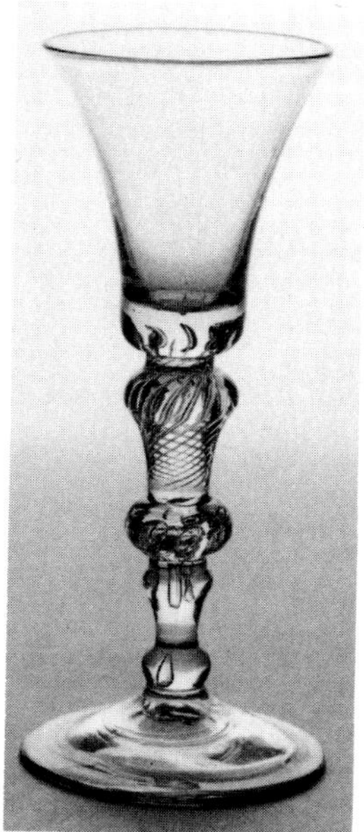

Right Composite stem wine glass with drawn bell bowl, multiple spiral air-twist stem with large shoulder knop and spiral extending into bowl, on a triple knop with tears and conical folded foot. 7¼in/18.3cm. £400–600.

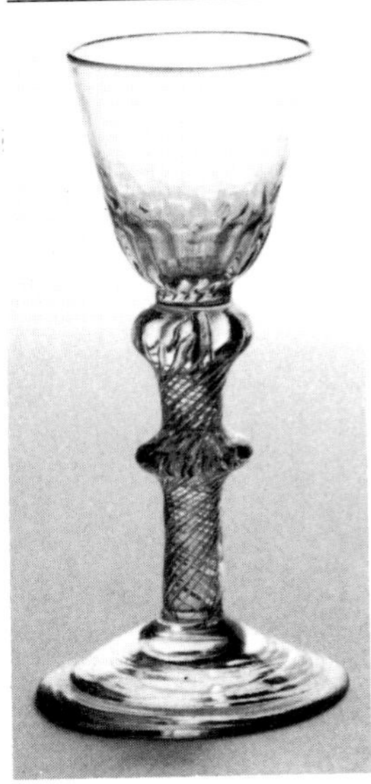

Wine glass with fluted round funnel bowl, the multiple spiral air-twist stem with shoulder and central knops, on conical foot, *c.*1750. 5⅝in / 14.5cm. £140–180.

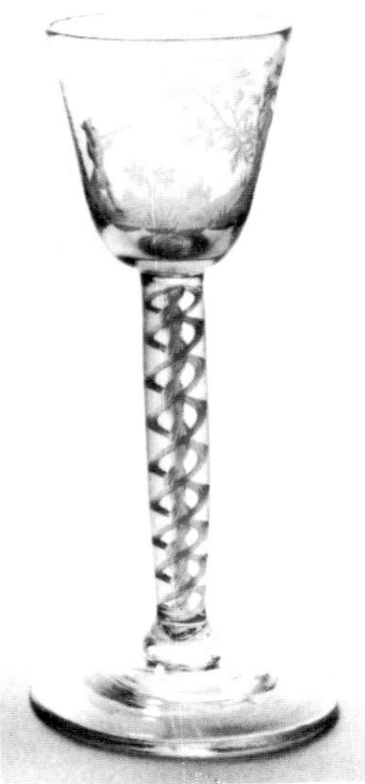

Wine glass with rounded funnel bowl engraved with hunting scene, stem with cable twist, on conical opaque foot. *c.*1760. 6⅛in / 15.7cm. £400–600.

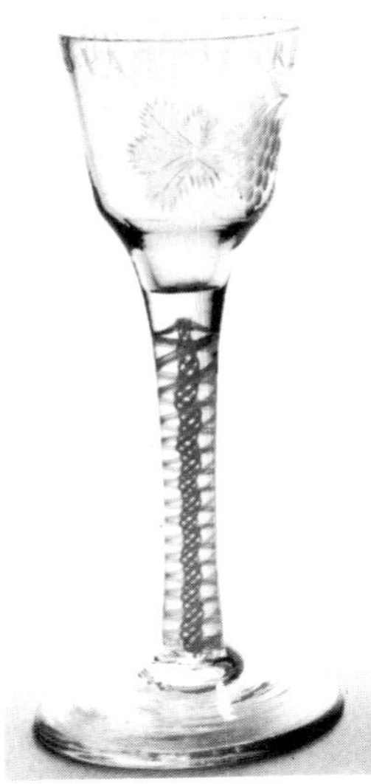

Electioneering glass with ogee bowl engraved with fruiting vine and 'Shafto & Vane Forever' with double series opaque twist stem on conical foot. 6⅛in / 15.7cm. £700–1000.

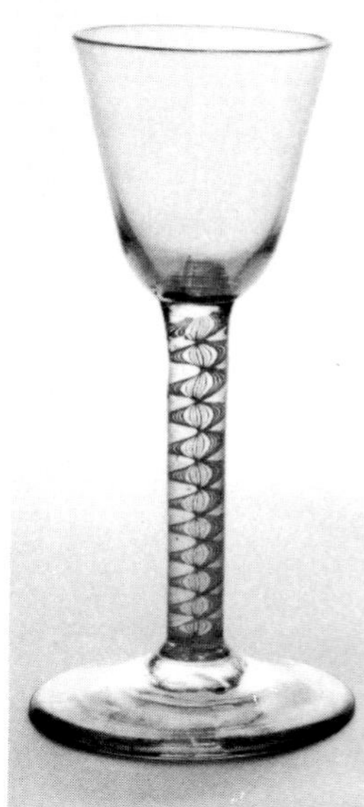

Rare colour twist wine glass with round funnel bowl, the stem with central six-ply canary yellow twist within a pair of six-ply opaque white corkscrews, on conical foot, *c.*1750–60. 6 in / 15 cm. £1500–2000.

Rare colour twist wine glass with round funnel bowl, the stem with central multi-ply opaque white corkscrew entwined by one red and one blue spiral thread, on conical folded foot, *c.*1750–60. 6 in / 15 cm. £900–1200.

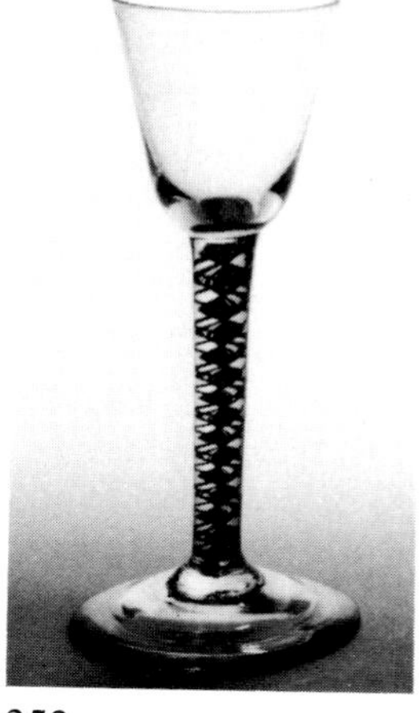

Wine glass with round funnel bowl with opaque white corkscrew twist with deep red and white spiral bands, on conical folded foot. 6⅛ in / 15.7 cm. £380–450.

'Jacobite' glasses

Jacobite wine glass with drawn trumpet bowl engraved with six-petalled rose, one bud and a leaf, on plain stem with tear, on folded conical foot, *c.*1740–50. 5½in/14cm. £350–450.

Wine glass with diamond-faceted stem and round funnel bowl engraved with six-petalled rose and leaves and two buds, on plain conical foot, *c.*1770. 6in/15cm. £200–300.

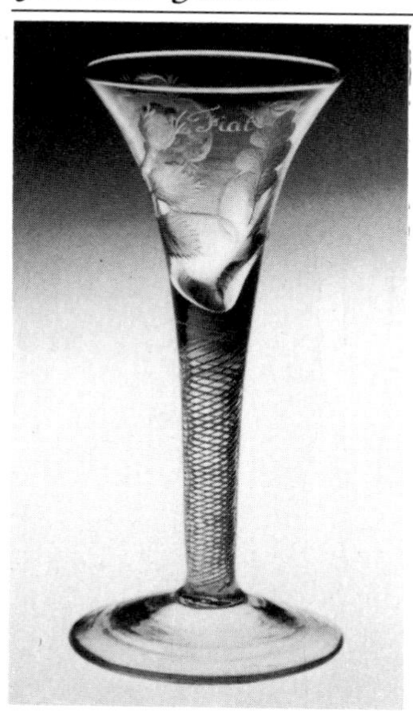

Jacobite glass, wheel-engraved with a rose, a half rose, a bud and an oak leaf inscribed 'Fiat' with an air-twist stem on conical foot, *c.*1745. 5⅝in/14.5cm. £450–550.

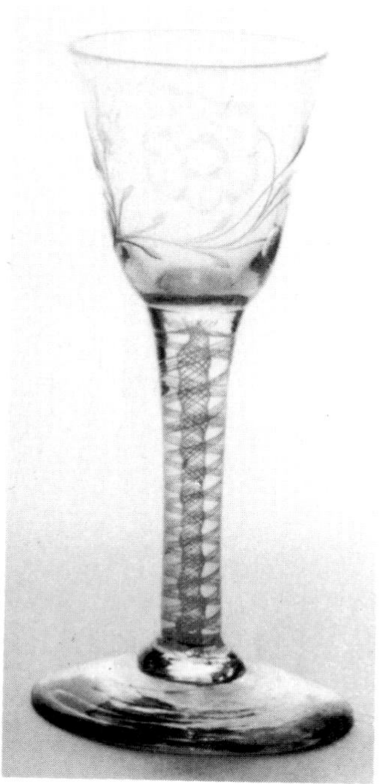

Wine glass engraved with six-petalled rose and bud and bird in flight with opaque twist stem on conical foot, *c.*1755. 5½in/14cm. £300–400.

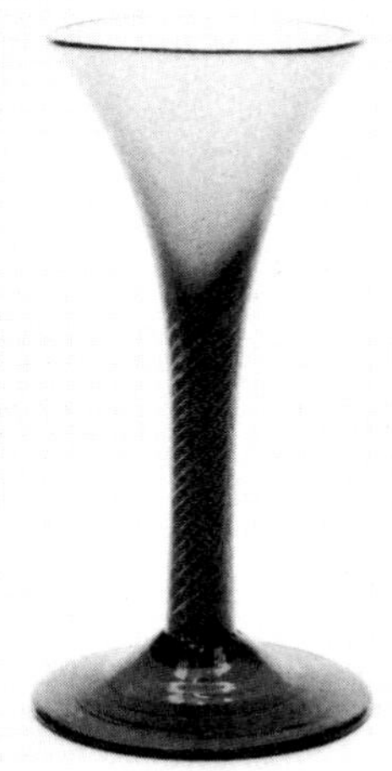

Wine glass with drawn trumpet bowl, green-tinted glass with multiple spiral air-twist stem on conical foot, *c.*1760. 7 in / 18 cm. £600–800.

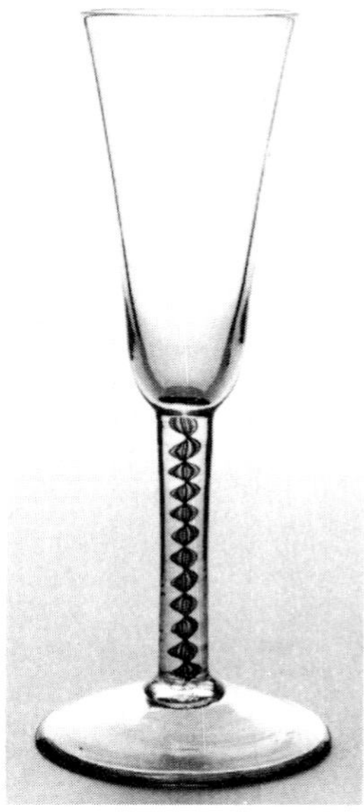

Ale glass with round funnel bowl and colour twist stem with threads of opaque white, blue and deep canary yellow, *c.*1760–70. 7⅞ in / 20 cm. £1300–1700.

Ale glass with tall round funnel bowl engraved with hops and barley, with opaque twist stem, *c.*1760. 6⅝ in / 17 cm. £200–250.

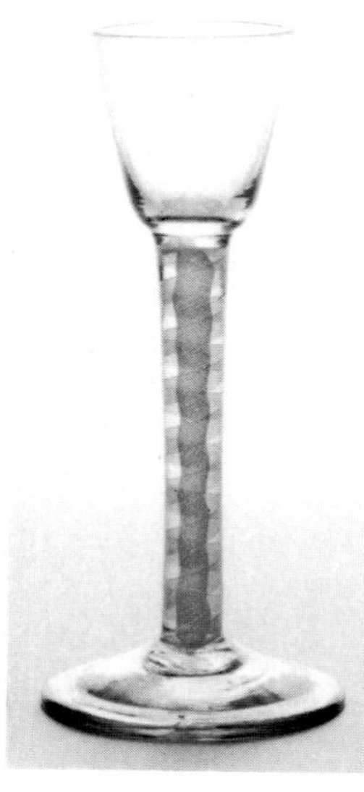

Cordial glass with round funnel bowl and opaque twist multi-ply band outside of a gauze, *c.*1750–60. 6 in / 15.5 cm. £200–250.

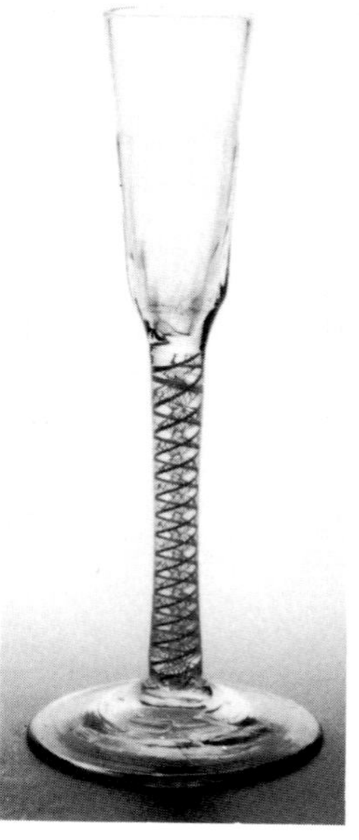

Ale glass with tall ogee bowl with basal fluting, on double series opaque twist stem, *c.*1760. 7⅛ in / 18.3 cm. £180–250.

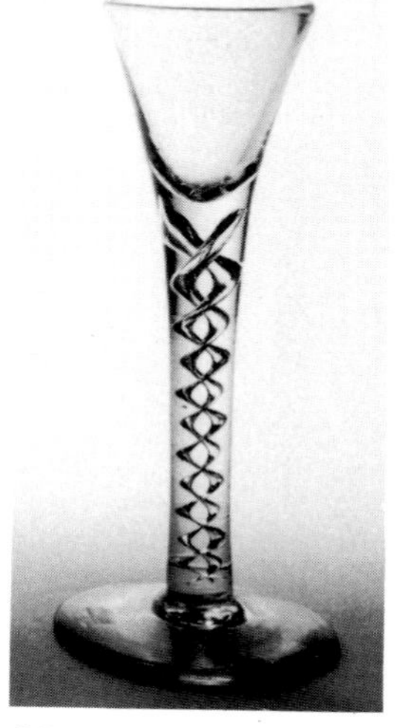

Cordial glass with drawn trumpet bowl and mercurial air-twist stem, *c.*1740–50. 6⅝ in / 17 cm. £200–300.

Wine glass with lipped round funnel bowl with basal cutting and hexagonal faceted stem, with lobed faceted foot, *c.*1775–80. 6 in / 15.5 cm. £100–140.

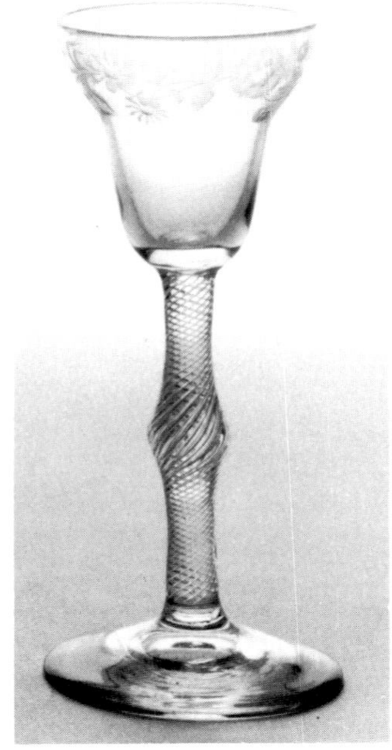

Wine glass with pan-topped bowl engraved with floral meander on multiple spiral air-twist stem with swelled knop, on plain conical foot, *c.*1760. 5½ in / 14 cm. £250–350.

An 18th-century German engraved glass tankard with pewter foot-rim and border, with pewter lid, dated 1763. £350–480.

An 18th-century German engraved glass tankard and cover with cut glass finial, dated 1790. £380–500.

Cameo glass

Stourbridge cameo glass vase in light olive green overlaid thinly in white, *c.*1880. 5 in / 12.5 cm. £400–600.

Below Cameo scent bottle, Stourbridge, with 'cracked ice' body overlaid in white and deep red, with silver mounts, *c.*1890. £600–800.

Stourbridge cameo glass oil lamp in white glass cased in deep raspberry red and overlaid with white, on three clear glass feet, *c.*1880–90. £600–800.

Thomas Webb cameo vase with yellow ground overlaid in white. Moulded mark, *c.*1880. 3½ in/8.9 cm. £300–400.

Thomas Webb 'four layer' cameo glass with white base cased in yellow, red and white, *c.*1880. 6 in/15.5 cm. £600–900.

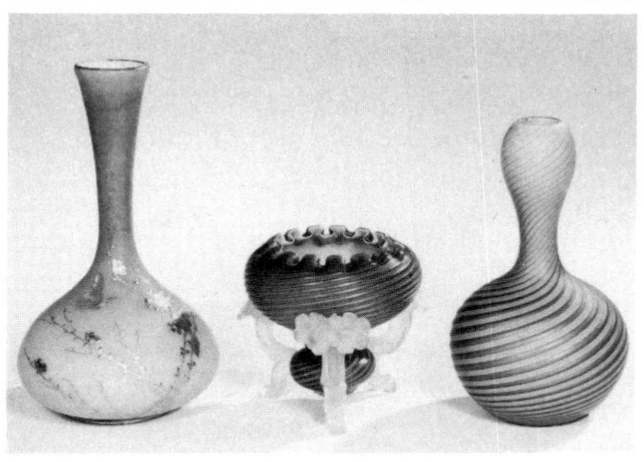

Left to right Stourbridge peachblow satin glass vase. £200–250. Stevens and Williams swirl satin bowl, £150–180, and vase, £200–250. All *c.*1880.

Stourbridge cameo glass scent bottle in deep pink overlaid with white narcissus, *c.*1880. 4¾in / 12cm. £450–550.

White 'opaline' vase painted in bright colours, *c.*1850. Probably made in Stourbridge by Richardsons. £500–800.

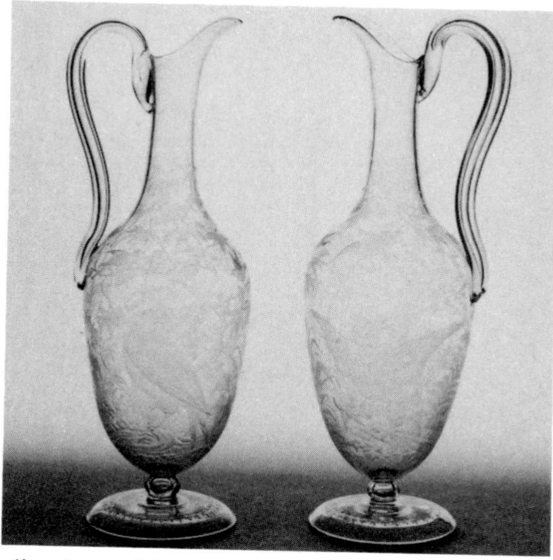

Above A pair of claret jugs in 'Rock Crystal' style, *c.*1870. £700–1000 single. *Below* 'Rock Crystal' style ewer, *c.*1870. £1800–2400.

Triple-overlay cameo glass vase with formalized flowers and leaves overlaid on matt ground. £480–600.

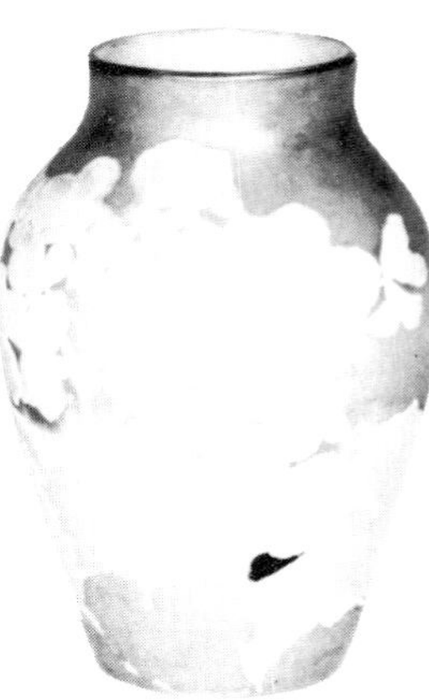

Glass vase of ovoid shape overlaid in pink and brown with brambles on a smokey pink ground, signed Gallé. £500–700.

Gallé cameo landscape vase overlaid in brown on a smokey matt background, the tall neck flaring towards the mouth. £300–400.

Fine large Lalique glass vase with metal mount, of 'Aigrettes' pattern. 9½in/24cm. £750–950.

Frosted glass figure 'Source de la Fontaine'. £1200–1500.

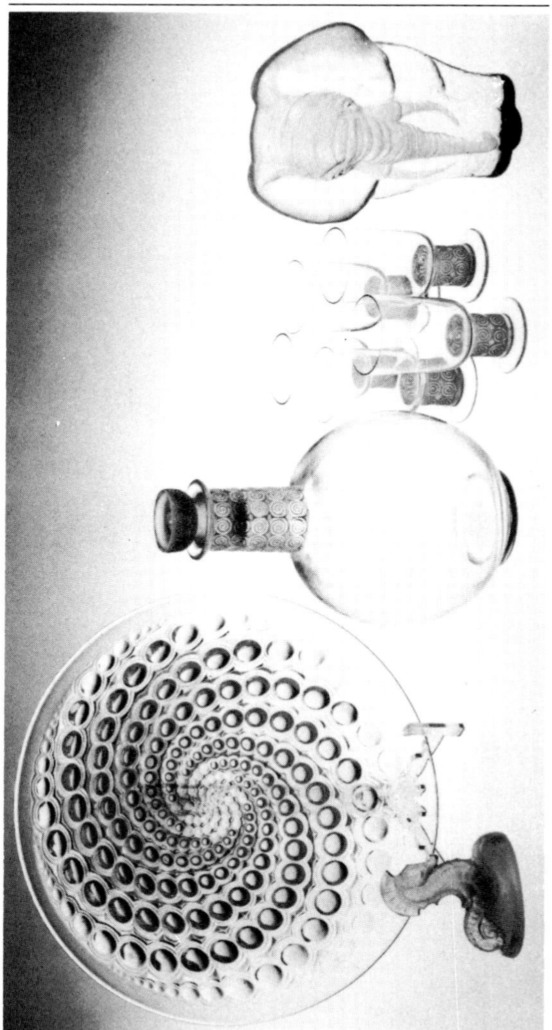

Lalique whirlpool moulded glass plate, plain spherical decanter with neck decorated with spirals, with matching glasses, a Swedish glass figure of a sea-horse, and a clear and frosted glass elephant, also Swedish. £750–850, £120–210, £50–70, £45–65.

Glossary

Acanthus Leaf pattern derived from Greek and Roman design.
Act of Parliament clock Large wall-clock with wooden face and short case, named after tax briefly imposed on clocks and watches in 1797.
Acid engraving, acid etching In glass, where acid is used to produce similar results to true engraving, but with thin shallow lines. In silver, a similar process.
Adam style Neo-classical style attributed largely to the Adam brothers from *c.*1750s.
Air-twist Glasses with stems drawn from air bubbles into spiralling threads.
Alloy A combination of two or more metals.
Ale glass Tall slender glass for drinking strong ale, not beer.
Amorini Little baroque figures of angelic boys, as distinct from cupids or cherubs.
Anchor escapement See Escapement.
Animalier Resembling an animal, as spouts of tea and coffee pots.
Anneal The process of heating and quenching metal to keep it malleable while being worked.
Anthemion Stylised honeysuckle motif from classical Greek ornament.
Apostle spoon Popular finial from medieval times onwards for spoons.
Applied, applied relief Ornament, decoration, made separately and added.
Apron Shaped ornamental piece between front legs of stand, chair, table, etc.
Arabesque Elaborately intertwined stylised foliage and flowers.
Arcade Arch-shaped decoration.
Ark A slope-lidded chest, originally made by an arkwright.
Armoire Continental term for clothes press or cupboard.
Armorial Coat of arms, crests, heraldic badges.
Assay, Assay Office Test or trial of metals for purity – the Assay Office carried out the tests.
Astragal Small half-round moulding or beading – also most common type of glazing bars for glass cabinet doors.
Aumbry Food storage cupboard with bars to doors for ventilation.
Automata Mechanically-operated clockwork devices.

Bachelor's chest Small chest of drawers with folding top opening out as writing surface.
Backplate Metal plate behind handles and drawer pulls. In

clocks the back plate of a movement, often beautifully engraved.

Bail handle Simple half-round swing handle or drawer pull.

Ball-and-claw Originally dragon's claw grasping pearl, adapted with eagle's claw and lion's paw for feet of cabriole legs.

Balloon back Waisted chairback.

Bamboo See Caneware.

Baluster Pillar with vase or pear-shaped swelling, as chair and table legs of late 17th and 18th century and as stems of drinking glasses from *c.*1680, also as shape of silver hollow ware.

Banding See Cross-banding.

Baroque Florid style originating on the Continent, evident in English design from *c.*1660–1730 and some silver of same period.

Basal knop Knop at base of stem.

Basalte Fine black stoneware developed from 'Egyptian black' by Josiah Wedgwood *c.*1760. Revived in 19th century as 'basalt'.

Bat Printing Development of over-glaze transfer-printing using a 'bat' or flexible sheet composed of glue, whiting and treacle.

Bayonet fitting Secure method of fixing pierced tops of dredgers to bases, as light bulbs fix into sockets.

Beading Continuous row of half-rounds like a bead necklace.

Bellarmine Originating in Germany, brownish salt-glazed stoneware flasks or bottles with relief mask, copied in England from 17th–19th century.

Bergere Low-backed chair with back and arms in continuous curve.

Bifurcated Forked.

Biggin Squat-shaped coffee pot with short pouring lip from *c.*1796, originally on stands with lamps.

Billet Thumbpiece on tankard or flagon.

Bilston enamel From *c.*1740 enamel made in the Birmingham/Bilston area.

Birdcage In clocks, the upright pillar construction holding the movement between two plates. In tables, a similar construction with hinge to allow table top to tilt, lift off or revolve.

Biscuit, bisque Once-fired unglazed porcelain ware.

Bleeding bowl Small shallow bowl with single handle or 'ear'.

Block front Cabinet doors with solid wooden panels and no glazing. Originally referred to solid wooden fronts on different planes, as breakfront.

Blown moulded In glass, vessels shaped by blowing glass into a metal mould. Used from 17th century onwards with one-piece moulds and from *c.*1800 with two-piece moulds when the inner surface was completely smooth and did not follow the contours of outside configurations.

Blue dash charger Dutch pattern Delftware with rims of plates, bowls, sponged with diagonal lines of blue suggesting ropework. Much copied in England in 17th and 18th century.

Bobbin turning, reel turning Turned uprights with continuous swell and ring shape like rounded cotton reels.

Body Any basic clay mix for earthenware and stoneware. In porcelain and bone china, called 'paste'.

Bolt and shutter Device to keep clock movement going when the shutter covering the winding hole is opened.

Glossary

Bombé French term for chests with swelling outline both vertically and horizontally.
Bone china From *c.*1794 the paste used for English tableware.
Bonheur du jour Light ladies' writing cabinet on four tall slender legs.
Boulle, Buhl Tortoiseshell and brass or silver marquetry made originally by André Charles Boulle (1642–1732). 'Premiere partie' is tortoiseshell inlaid with metal, 'contre partie' is metal inlaid with tortoiseshell.
Bow front Furniture with convex curve horizontally.
Bracket clock Spring-driven clocks without long pendulums made to stand on a table or shelf.
Bracket foot Shaped like a wooden shelf bracket, used on chests and cabinets, etc.
Braganza scroll Rather ornate, compressed S-scroll.
Bramah lock Barrel lock used on English furniture from *c.*1784.
Break front Furniture with the central section stepped slightly forward.
Bright cut Technique of engraving with minutely faceted cutting, much used in silver in latter part of 18th century.
Britannia standard Higher ratio of pure silver metal in silver plate enforced from 1697–1720, marked with a figure of Britannia seated.
British plate Variation of Sheffield plate using nickel alloy instead of copper as the core, patented in 1836.
Broken pediment Pediment broken in centre sometimes with pedestal for urn, bust or decorative feature.
Brushing slide Pull-out surface just below top of chest of drawers and above top drawer.
Bull's eye In clocks, the small glass aperture through which the pendulum can be seen in a longcase clock. In glass, the thickened centre of a sheet of Crown glass.
Bull's eye stopper Distinctive shape of decanter stopper, disc-shaped with wavy edge, thinning to a hole in centre.
Bun foot Ball-shaped foot to furniture, common in late 17th century and revived by Victorians.
Burmese glass Opaque heat-shaded glass toning from pale yellow to deep pink, made by Thomas Webb & Sons under US patent.
Burnished Gold, silver or gilding polished with hardstone to give a brilliant finish.
Burr Veneer cut from the root with distinctive figure and patterning.

Cabaret set In bone china, more rarely porcelain, teaset for one or two people, including a matching tray.
Cabinet ware Decorative ceramics of high artistic standard for display only, not for use.
Cabriole leg Shape of furniture leg based on cyma curve, using spring of solid wood cut away to curve outwards at knee, tapering slightly and curving inwards above the foot.
Calyx Cup-like shape of leaves enclosing bud or flower.
Cameo glass Two-colour glass with white over dark base, the white, cut or acid-etched to varying degrees of thickness.
Campagna Bell-shaped Greek vase, a shape popular in neo-classical designs of Regency period.
Candle slide Small pull-out tray to hold candlestick.
Cane In glass, coloured or opaque rods used in making

colour-twist glasses and paperweights.
Caneware In ceramics, straw-coloured dry stoneware developed by Josiah Wedgwood, used for making tableware and bamboo-ware.
Canted corner A corner cut off diagonally, on a slanting plane, on chests, cabinets, etc.
Capstan Cylindrical shape curving inwards at the waist.
Carcase Basic structure of a piece of furniture, often in cheaper wood, then veneered.
Carlton House desk Writing table with D-shaped superstructure, on tapering legs, of late 18th-century design.
Carolean Applied to designs of Charles I and Charles II periods.
Cartel clock Ornate French wall clock adapted in England with giltwood frames instead of ormolu.
Cartouche Framework or surround to coat of arms or crest. The term also used to describe similar-shaped frame enclosing decorative motif.
Cased glass Glass overlaid with one or more colours, one of which was usually white, and cut away to show colour beneath. Also called 'flashed' glass.
Cast Solid metal made in a mould, as distinct from sheet metal.
Caster Container with perforated top for sprinkling sugar, pepper, etc.
Castor Small wheel set in brass socket or between brass arms on base of furniture.
Cellarette Compartmented container to hold wine bottles, from Georgian period onwards.
Chamber stick Candle holder on low stem set in wide dish, often with slot for snuffers or extinguisher cap.
Chamfered Similar to 'canted' but of legs of tables, chairs, etc.
Charger Large deep-bowled serving dish.
Chased, chasing Decoration in high or low relief using blunt tools to shape metal, often used in conjunction with embossing. No metal is removed in process, unlike engraving. Flat-chasing is the decorating of a surface using this technique instead of engraving.
Chiffonier Low side cabinet with shelves or doors below a marble top.
Chiming clock A clock chiming quarters as well as hours.
China stone Ingredient of hard-paste porcelain.
Chinese lattice Geometric asymmetrical lattice, sometimes called 'cracked ice'.
Chinoiserie Recurring fashion for European versions of Oriental designs.
Chip carving Shallow, geometric carving on early English oak furniture.
Cobalt Blue pigment used for ceramic decoration and 'Bristol blue' coloured glass.
Cockbead Small usually half-round mouldings, generally round drawer-fronts from *c.*1730.
Cockshead hinge S-shaped hinge, originally in iron, later in brass.
Coffee can Straight-sided mug-shaped cup.
Coffered panel A panel which is sunk in its frame, opposite of 'fielded'.
Collar Small moulding around vertical part of piece of furniture, usually table legs. Also called 'gaitered'.

Commode From the French, an elegant chest on short legs made in England from *c.*1740.
Contre partie See Boulle.
Console Table fixed to the wall and supported on decorative front bracket legs.
Cordial glass Small-bowled drinking glass for strong aromatic drinks similar to liqueurs.
Cornice Decorative or plain moulding below the pediment.
Cottages Pastille burners, money boxes, souvenirs, made in bone china or Staffordshire pottery.
Count wheel A wheel in the striking mechanism of a clock.
Court cupboard From the 16th century an open cupboard for displaying plate, often wrongly called a 'buffet'.
Cow's horn stretcher See Crinoline stretcher.
Crabstock Handles of tea and coffee pots shaped like a gnarled crab-apple branch.
Cracked ice See Chinese lattice.
Creamware Developed by Josiah Wedgwood from *c.*1760 from yellow-buff clays with cream-coloured glaze *c.*1764 making it non-porous and hardwearing.
Credence table Small flap side table opening to a circular or hexagonal top.
Credenza From late medieval period, a cupboard for storing food, hence an Italian side-cupboard, often ornately decorated.
Crest rail Top horizontal rail of a chairback.
Crinoline stretcher Half-hoop stretcher common on Windsor chairs.
Cross-banding Strips of veneer edging table tops, drawer fronts, etc. cut across the grain to prevent lifting and shrinking.
Cullet Broken glass melted down for cost-cutting reasons in glass-making.
Cushion drawer Drawer with no pulls in cornice of escritoires, late 17th and early 18th century.
Cut card work Decoration on silver using thin sheets of silver cut into shapes of foliage, scrolls, etc. and applied (soldered) on to vessels to produce relief ornament without casting from *c.*1660 onwards.
Cutlery Any eating implement with a cutting edge.
Cyma curve Also known as ogee, ogive, an S-shaped curve, concave above, convex below.
Cymric silver Made for Liberty & Co mainly with mechanical processes for decorative 'Art Nouveau' objects.

Davenport Small, low, compact ladies' desk made from *c.*1789.
Deceptive glass Small glass with thickened bowl for making small drinks look larger, i.e. for Toastmasters.
Delftware English earthenware associated with Delft, Holland.
Demilune Half circular.
Dentil Cornice moulding with repeating raised rectangular blocks like teeth.
Dial plate The whole part of a clock face on which the chapter ring and spandrels are fixed.
Diamond-point engraving Engraving with a fine diamond-pointed tool on glass to achieve a stippled effect.
Diaper Repeated lozenge, diamond or trellis design.
Dish ring Hollow, waisted cylinder in silver and other metals to hold warm plates and dishes clear of polished surfaces. As

'potato ring' it was placed on a dish lined with a napkin and filled with jacket potatoes.

Dished Concave shaping, on solid wooden chair seats, candle slides, on games tables to hold counters.

Distressed Trade term for damaged piece of furniture or surface.

Douter Cone-shaped candle extinguisher.

Dowel Wooden peg used to secure frame of furniture.

Dram glass Small glass with heavy foot and short thick stem holding 2oz spirits.

Drawn stem, bowl In glasses where the stem and bowl are made in one part and not separately when it is known as 'stuck shank'.

Draw-leaf table, draw table Table extending with two leaves which pull out from beneath central section.

Dredger Correctly, a kitchen caster with a loop handle, but term also used for sugar casters, etc.

Drop-in seat Seat of chair made with separate wooden frame.

Dumb waiter Two or three small circular tiers on a central tripod pillar.

Dummy drawer A mock drawer, usually to match up one on the opposite side, so appearing to be a pair.

Earthenware Clay wares which are porous after firing and therefore need glazing.

Ebonised Painted or stained to resemble ebony.

Electroplate Base metal coated with a thin layer of pure silver by electro-chemical galvanic action, from *c.*1840.

Electrotype Costly process using similar process to electroplating to reproduce rare original casts – also known as electro-forming, patented 1841.

Embossing Technique of raising relief decoration by hammering and punching sheet metal on a bed of pitch, usually finished more crisply on the outer surface, a process known as repoussé.

Enamel Clear glass, coloured or made opaque with pigments which subsequently fuses to the surface of glass, ceramics or metal.

Encaustic Decoration achieved by burning-in pigments to earthenware.

Engine-turned Close line patterns incised on fine stoneware or silver using a lathe.

Entrée dish Serving dish in silver, Cheffield plate, ceramics, with close-fitting lid.

Epergne Table centrepiece, frequently ornate, consisting of tiers of dishes on a central frame from which hang small baskets and dishes, from *c.*1760 onwards.

EPNS Electro-plated nickel silver.

Escapement The mechanism of a clock which allows the train to move at regular intervals. Anchor escapement from *c.*1670 allowed a long pendulum to swing in a narrow arc. Verge escapement has a crown wheel with teeth which allow the escape to pass at regular intervals, used with short bob pendulums.

Escutcheon Keyhole plate – also a shield shape for armorials.

Ewer Tall jug on pedestal foot.

Facet, facet cutting Shallow hollows ground or cut in stems,

etc. of glasses to make diamond pattern.
Façon de Venise Intricate vessels and objects made in fragile soda glass in Murano from 13th century onwards, imitated in England in 19th century.
Fall front A desk or bureau with a downward-hinging writing surface.
False pendulum Small disc attached to pendulum where it passes aperture in dial, set above pendulum itself.
Famille rose, famille vert Chinese porcelain in colours dominated by soft pink or green, the term adopted by English potteries from *c.*1720.
Fan cut Glass cut in fan shapes.
Felspar porcelain From *c.*1800 developed by Spode to modify bone china with pure felspar to produce brilliantly white, extremely hard wares.
Festoon An altogether lighter version of a swag.
Fiddle pattern Back splat of chair, terminal of silver flatware shaped like a violin.
Fielded panel Panel with bevelled or chamfered edges, the centre standing out in the frame.
Filled Another term for loaded.
Finial Top ornament, i.e. urn, flambeau, etc. on top of furniture, lids of silver and porcelain, clocks, etc.
Fire polishing Reheated moulded glass polished to remove mould marks thereby suggesting hand-cut or blown work.
Firing glass Glass used for toasts accompanied by rapping on the table like gunfire – thick and stumpy with heavy stem and disc foot, from *c.*1760 onwards.
Flatware In silverware, all tableware without a cutting edge. In porcelain, plates and flat dishes as distinct from hollow ware.
Flambeau Spiralling flame shape.
Flashing See Casing.
Flint glass Developed by George Ravenscroft *c.*1685, a pure brilliant glass containing lead oxide, also called lead crystal.
Flute glass Drinking glass with deep conical bowl on slender stem, for drinking cider or strong ale.
Fluted, fluting Close-set grooves, as on classical pillars.
Fly bracket Small brackets supporting narrow leaves of tables.
Folded foot Glass with domed or conical foot with outside rim turned under.
Foliate Pattern or design with leaves.
Fret, fretted Openwork pattern, usually geometrical.
Frieze, frieze drawer In furniture, the horizontal part below a cabinet cornice or below a table top. The frieze drawer is set below the table top in the frieze.
Fruitwood Wood from orchard trees such as apple and pear.
Fusee In clocks, the cone-shaped piece of metal with a spiral track, round which the gut or chain winds as it comes off the spring barrel.

Gadroon Repetitive lobes either upright or slanting, suggesting the knuckles of a clenched fist.
Gaitered See Collar.
Gallery Raised border or miniature balustrade in wood or metal.
Garniture Set of three or more decorative urns, vases, for a mantel or cabinet.

Gate leg The hinged legs and stretchers which pivot out from the main frame of a table to support the hinged flaps or leaves.
Gilt metal Base metal which has been gilded, not necessarily ormolu.
Glaze Coating of glass-like transparency making earthenware non-porous and fusing to the body or paste of porcelain to fix the decoration beneath.
Glazing bars The bars holding panes of glass into a door of a cabinet.
Gothic A style associated with medieval German design, of pointed arches and pinnacles.
Grande sonnerie A clock chiming or striking both hour and quarter hour every quarter.
Great wheel In clock movements, the first wheel of the going train.
Greek key, Greek fret Rigidly stylised wave pattern composed of straight lines.
Green glaze ware Developed by Josiah Wedgwood for table ware particularly in leaf shapes from *c.*1764.
Grille Lattice of brass wire.
Guilloche Repeating ornament of intertwined ribbons making a series of small circles.

Hall chair, seat With solid wooden seat and back, often painted with armorials.
Hallmark Assay Office mark signifying that silver has come up to standard of purity.
Harlequin set A set of tableware with each piece in the same design but a different colour or pattern.
Harlequin table Version of the Pembroke table with small rising section containing pigeonholes and drawers.
Hard-paste porcelain 'True' porcelain first made in England at Plymouth *c.*1768 but difficult to work and soon superseded by bone china.
Heavy baluster First series of baluster-stemmed wine glasses made from *c.*1680.
Hobnail cutting Pattern of cut glass with deep incisions, cross-cut to form eight-pointed stars.
Hollow ware In all table ware, hollow vessels as opposed to flatware.
Hood In clocks, the upper removable part of a longcase clock enclosing the dial.
Huguenot French Protestants fleeing from the Revocation of the Edict of Nantes in 1685, including many fine craftsmen and silversmiths escaping to England from religious persecution.

Imari pattern 18th-century Japanese export porcelain much copied in English 'Japan pattern' by Worcester, Derby, etc.
'Improve' Later Victorian decoration to mainly 18th-century silver and furniture.
Incised ornament Cut, carved or engraved as opposed to 'applied'.
Inlay Decorative patterns cut in surface of solid wood and inset with contrasting woods, metals, ivory, etc.
'In the white' Once-fired porcelain often decorated by artists outside the pottery or factory.
Ironstone china Patented by C. J. Mason in 1813, strong white hard-wearing earthenware, slightly transparent and heavy.

Jacobite Engraving, painting, supporting the cause of the Old and Young Pretenders, particularly the 1745 Rebellion.
Japanning A finish composed of layers of varnish on coloured grounds decorated with 'chinoiserie' on English furniture, clock cases.
Japan pattern See Imari, Kakiemon.
Jasper ware Dense fine stoneware needing no glaze introduced by Josiah Wedgwood *c.*1774, tinted throughout the body in pale blue, green, lilac. Later imitations were 'jasper dip' with colour on surface from dipping in jasper slip.

Kakiemon Design of Chinese origin adapted by Japanese potters, patterns widely copied by English potters.
Knee In chairs, tables, etc. the top of the leg which curves outwards.
Knop In glass, decorative shapes on stems – acorn, mushroom, cushion, etc. In silver, decorative finial cast and soldered to straight handles of early spoons.
Kylin Japanese dragon device used in pottery and porcelain patterns and as decorative handles.

Lacquer Should only describe Japanese work, but in general covers English Japanning as well.
Lambeth Delft General name for London-made Delftware.
Lancet clock Regency bracket clock shape with Gothic pointed arched case.
Lantern clock Early weight-driven clock made from *c.*1630–*c.*1730 with posted 'birdcage' frame and brass case topped by a single bell.
Late-embossed In silver, earlier wares which have been embossed at a later date, usually Victorian.
Latticino In glass, ancient technique of enclosing fine threads of opaque or coloured glass in clear glass – used to describe Nailsea glass with trailed white decoration.
Lead glass See Flint glass.
Lenticle Proper term for 'bull's eye' aperture in the waist door of a longcase clock.
Light baluster Taller, slimmer version of heavy baluster glass typified by 'Newcastle' glasses.
Linenfold Formal representations of folds of cloth on carved panels from late 15th century, revived 19th century.
Lion's mask Decorative motif used in silver and on furniture mounts, particularly drawer pulls.
Lip moulding Similar to thumb moulding.
Loaded Sheet metal filled with pitch, e.g. silver and Sheffield plate candlesticks.
Lopers Supports to fall-fronts, brushing slides, etc.
Low relief Carved or embossed decoration projecting only slightly from the surface.
Lunar dial On clocks, the dial showing phases of the moon.
Lunette Half-moon shaped decoration.
Lustre ware Generally describes pottery from Staffordshire and Sunderland decorated with metallic salts and fired to give gold, silver or copper-like finish.
Lyre end, lyre back Shaped like a musical lyre.

Maintaining power In clocks, a device to keep the movement going while being wound. See Bolt and shutter.

Majolica, Maiolica Early Italian tin-glazed earthenware similar to Delft. The anglicised 'majolica' generally applies to brightly-coloured relief-moulded wares developed by Minton *c.*1851.
Marquetry Decorative patterns inset into a single sheet of veneer cut to receive the different coloured pieces.
'Marriage' Trade term for piece of furniture made up from parts of similar pieces, i.e. bureau, bookcase, etc.
Marrow scoop Long narrow scoop in heavy-gauge silver for scooping marrow from bones, sometimes combined with a spoon.
Martinware Salt-glazed stoneware 'grotesques' and other ware made by the Martin Brothers at Southall *c.*1877–1915.
Mask Decorative motif derived from classical masks worn in Greek theatre.
Master glass Sweetmeat glass at the top of a table centrepiece, sometimes called Orange glass.
Matt, matting In silver and on clock faces, small punch-marks covering surface giving textured finish.
Mazarine In silver and ceramics a strainer dish pierced in decorative patterns, placed beneath a fish to drain juices, less frequently beneath fowl or joint.
Mazarine blue Rich dark blue, applied to soft-paste porcelain biscuit.
Mean time Time recorded by mechanical methods giving hours of equal length.
Meissen German porcelain factory near Dresden which first made hard-paste porcelain successfully in Europe *c.*1710.
Mercury twist Air-twist stems incorporating canes of exceptionally brilliant glass resembling mercury.
Milled In silver, finished like the rims of coins.
Millefiore Ornamental glass, usually paperweights, made using canes of many-coloured glass.
Mons In porcelain, centre of a dish, plate or bowl, usually slightly raised.
Monteith Large silver bowl with detachable notched or scalloped rim for holding wine glasses by their stems with their their bowls in iced water.
Mortise and tenon In furniture, joining end-grain to side grain with a tongue slotting into second piece, usually at right angles, secured by pegs or dowels.
Mote spoon Long-handled spoon with pierced bowl and pointed end for skimming poured tea and unblocking spout strainer of teapot.
Moulded In glass and ceramics, blown, pressed or cast in a mould. In furniture, decoratively shaped sections of applied ornament are known as 'mouldings'.
Mount Term usually used to describe metals used in association with other materials in a decorative form.
Murano Venetian glass-making centre from 13th century.

Nailsea glass Fancy glass including rolling pins, walking sticks, gemmel flasks in imitation 'latticino' – inaccurate descriptive term.
Nankin blue Name for ancient capital of China from which great quantities of blue-and-white wares were exported to England.
Nottingham ware Heavy, functional, brown stoneware.

Octafoil Eight lobed, as in 'trefoil'.
Ogee, Ogive See cyma curve.
Opal, opaline Semi-opaque glass with fiery glow like gemstone.
Ormolu Bronze fire-gilded with powdered gold in elaborately decorative furniture mounts, clock cases, etc. English equivalent is usually gilt brass or gilt metal.
Overlay Glass cased or 'flashed' in different colours.
Ovolo Convex moulding of quarter-round section.
Oyster veneer Veneer cut from small branches with fine figuring and grain, resembling oyster shells.

Pad foot Simple rounded out-turned foot to furniture.
Palladian Style of architecture based on classical Roman by Andrea Palladio in 16th century greatly influencing early Georgian and Adam design.
Parcel gilt Partially gilded, usually of silver.
Parian ware Vitrified porcelain simulating white Grecian marble from Paros made from *c.*1842 for portrait busts, shaped in moulds.
Parquetry Veneers cut in geometrical patterns, as in 'parquet floor'.
Paste Substance forming the 'body' of porcelain.
Pastille burner Small model, usually of cottage or summer house in bone china or pottery, in which aromatic pastilles were burned.
Patera Small circular ornament, flat or in low relief.
Pâte-sur-pâte Similar technique in ceramics to cameo glass, with white semi-transparent slip over a coloured ground, pared or cut away to show tones of body colour.
Patina Build-up of centuries' gloss and polish from use and wear.
Paw foot Shaped like a lion's paw.
Pearlware Tough white earthenware with faint translucence called by J. Wedgwood 'an improvement on creamware' and ideal for transfer-printing.
Pedestal foot, base Solid base to furniture without feet, but shaped like the base of a pedestal.
Pediment The topmost part of cabinet furniture above the cornice.
Pegged Fixed, as in mortise and tenon joints, with pegs or dowels.
Petite sonnerie Striking on two bells of different tones to denote each quarter, also known as 'ting tang strike'.
Petuntse Ingredient of hard-paste porcelain.
Piecrust In furniture, silver, rims carved in a series of cyma curves.
Piecrust ware Made by Wedgwood *c.*1770 to resemble standing pies, copied by other potteries from 1830s onwards.
Pierced Openwork decoration in silver, wood, etc.
Pillar In clocks, the upright posts supporting the front and back plates of the movement.
Pillar-and-claw Originally described small tripod stands for tables, etc., now also for pillar supports for dining tables.
Pitch Resinous tarry substance used for 'filling' or 'loading' candlesticks, and as working base on which silversmiths could chase and emboss.
Planishing Smoothing, polishing surface of finished silver by hammering with slightly convex planishing hammer.

Plated Of silver, generally implies electro-plated.
'Plate' The name by which all articles in silver and gold are known.
Plates In clocks, the two flat metal pieces which contain the movement.
Plinth Square or rectangular base to furniture.
Polychrome Many colours.
Pontil Dab of molten glass used to fix glass vessels to a rod during finishing. Pontil mark is the uneven break mark where the pontil has been snapped off.
Porcelain White paste as opposed to earthenware body.
Porringer Two-handled cup with or without lid and saucer, in silver, pottery and porcelain in all shapes and sizes, for semi-solid gruels, etc. A 'caudle cup' is strictly speaking for liquids.
Posted movement, frame In clocks, where the plates are horizontal and held by four or more corner pillars or posts.
Prattware Made by many potters from *c.*1790–1830s, brightly-coloured pottery, jugs, figures, etc., now generally attribute to Felix Pratt.
Premiere partie See Boulle.
Press A large cupboard for linen, clothes, etc.
Press moulded Thick, heavy glass in imitation of cut glass introduced from *c.*1830, finished by fire-polishing with legitimate use of pontil, not intended to suggest old glass.
Provenance History of an antique and proof of previous ownership.
Provincial clock Made anywhere outside London.
Prunt Small applied decoration to early drinking glasses, often called 'strawberry prunt' because of their shape.
Pseudo oriental, Chinese Mock character marks on Oriental style porcelain.
Pull repeat, push repeat Clocks with striking mechanisms activated at any time by pulling a cord or pushing a button.
Punched, punched work Decoration round rim of silver punched from the back to raise rows of hollow beading.
Putti Small cherubs, cupids, on Baroque and Renaissance designs.

Quarter veneer Veneer laid in four quarters instead of a single piece.
Quartetto tables Four small tables in graduated sizes fitting into each other.
'Queen Anne' Style covering period 1700–20 and revived in 19th century, now generally called 'Queen Anne Style'.

Rack strike Mechanism of a clock striking train activated by a serrated wheel, introduced 1676.
Rail In furniture, horizontal parts of a frame – e.g. crest rail of a chair.
Raising In silversmithing, the making of hollow ware by hammering and shaping on a 'raising stake'.
Ratafia glass Tall flute glass of small capacity for almond-flavoured cordial.
Reeding Parallel close-set convex moulding, the opposite of fluting.
Regulator (clock) Weight-driven pendulum clock with no striking mechanism with dead-beat escapement and compensating pendulum for extremely accurate timekeeping.
Repoussé See Chasing, Embossing.

Reserve, reserving In ceramics, the part of the decoration not covered by the ground colour.
Ring-turned Rings round columns, stems, legs, made on a lathe.
Rise and fall dial Small dial on clock face for raising and lowering pendulum thus regulating speed of movement.
Rising top Term originally used by 18th-century and 19th-century cabinet-makers for part of furniture which rose by mechanical means, now generally for any part of superstructure additional to basic design.
Roemer German glass with wide hollow stem for drinking Rhenish wines, usually pale green in colour.
Rope twist Decorative device to commemorate Nelson's victories from *c.*1805.
Rummer Deep-bowled English glass on short stem with wide foot for drinking rum punches.

Sabre leg Chair leg with concave curve in the shape of a scimitar or sabre.
Salt-glaze Non-porous glaze achieved by throwing salt into pottery kiln at maximum temperature so that it vitrifies.
Salver A small tray on a single central foot.
Scale, salmon scale Small design resembling fish scales used extensively in Worcester porcelain patterns to break up areas of dark blue grounds, less frequently pink, from *c.*1760.
Scallop, Scalloped In the shape of a shell, with a rim indented like a sea shell.
Scratch blue Scratched or incised ornament with colour showing only in incisions.
Sealtop Cast finial of early spoons with flat top resembling a sealing-wax seal.
Seat board The wooden board on which the movement rests in longcase clocks.
Seaweed marquetry Patterns of intricate scrolling veneer.
Secretaire Fitted writing compartment with hinged fall-front, sometimes pulling out like a drawer. Also the whole piece of writing furniture incorporating this desk fitting.
Serpentine Front of furniture with horizontal S-curve.
Sèvres Famous French porcelain factory succeeding Vincennes in 1756, producing hard-paste porcelain from *c.*1772, soft-paste earlier.
Sgraffito See Scratch blue.
Sham See Dummy.
Sheffield plate Method of coating a copper core with thin layer of sterling silver, heat-fused and then worked like silver, with cut edges masked with great skill. From *c.*1742.
Sheveret Narrow writing tables with drawers and pigeon holes similar but more sturdy to bonheur du jour.
Shoe The brass fitting on furniture leg into which castor was fixed.
Shoulder knop The first knop below the bowl of a glass, or the socket of a candlestick.
Side chair Made to stand against a wall, armless chair usually slightly lower and wider than dining chair.
Silesian stem In glass, cut or shaped with four, six or eight sides tapering inwards below pronounced shoulder knop.
Sinking Shaping a piece of sheet silver by hammering in a hollowed out wooden block into a bowl shape.
Slice cutting Deep V-shaped incisions in glass.

Slipware Coarse earthenware covered or decorated with slip, watered-down potters' clay.
Smith's blue Brilliant blue underglaze named after its developer.
Snap-top Table with top which hinges from horizontal to vertical secured by small snap-hinge.
Snuffers Scissor-like implement with small box on one blade for extinguishing and trimming wicks of candles.
Soapstone porcelain Soft-paste porcelain with a steatite content, hot-water resistant and tougher than soft-paste porcelain.
Soda glass Used by Venetians, quick-cooling malleable glass often straw coloured or green tinged, and bubbled, more fragile than English flint glass.
Soft-paste porcelain White, translucent paste made in England from *c.*1740s.
Spade foot Square-sectioned tapering foot.
Spandrel Corner-piece, usually decorative, on clocks, furniture.
Spill jar Wide-mouthed often straight-sided vase.
Spindle turned Wood tapering at either end, swelling slightly in centre.
Spire cut In the shape of a church spire or steeple.
Splat Central vertical piece of chairback, often with decorative shape, ornament.
Splash enamel Opaque or coloured enamel splashed on to glass while still in molten state.
Spun silver Method of cheap, swift shaping of thin-gauge objects in silver and other metals, mainly 19th century.
Staffordshire Pottery from main centre of British pottery industry, loose term for brightly-painted earthenware and flat-backed mantel ornaments.
Sterling silver Pure silver alloyed with small quantity of copper to the standard required by Assay Offices.
Staved Decoration, construction, like a fence.
Stipple engraving See Diamond-point engraving.
Stirrup cup Round-based cup, usually in the shape of fox's head or other animal, used by mounted horsemen before a hunt.
Stoneware Earthenware mixed with sand or flint and fired at a higher temperature, making it non porous and strong.
Stourbridge glass Usually refers to glass made after *c.*1845 when new industrial glass centre was Stourbridge, noted for glassmaking from 17th century onwards.
Strapwork Low relief applied or carved, of scrolls, arabesques, geometric motifs, and in silver, applied ornament.
Stretcher Horizontal rails between the legs of tables, chairs, to give extra stability and strength.
Strike/silent Small lever or dial on clock face for regulating strike mechanism.
Strawberry dish Small saucer-like bowl, usually with fluted sides.
Stringing Narrow strips of wood or brass inlaid in wood. In glass, glass threads wound in spirals round stems, handles, etc.
Stuff-over Furniture frame, seat frame, covered with upholstery.
Sulphide glass Small china clay portraits in low relief embedded in brilliant flint glass, developed by Apsley Pellatt *c.*1819.
Sunderland Centre of earthenware pottery, known for

making nautical and marine commemorative ware, mainly 19th century.
Sunray veneer Cut in narrow triangular sections resembling rays of sun.
Swag Heavy curve of drapery, fruit, flowers.

Tallboy Double chest of drawers made in two parts from *c.*1710.
Tambour Flexible desk top or sliding cabinet door made of upright concave batons glued to thick fabric.
Tapered Narrowing towards the base.
Tazza From Italian meaning 'cup' on a tall stem. Misused as a type of silver tray or salver.
Tear drop Bubble of air entrapped in stem of glass.
Terminal Literally the end, usually of decorative socket or base of handle, etc.
Thumb moulding Flattened half-round moulding on edges of furniture, round drawer fronts.
Timepiece Any clock with no striking mechanism.
Tin enamel, tin glaze Once-fired earthenware dipped in lead glaze mixed with tin oxide giving a smooth white finish.
Toastmaster's glass Glass with thick bowl to exaggerate quantity of liquor.
Tower clock, turret clock Large clocks made for steeples, churches, stable buildings, etc.
Train The wheels and pinions forming the movement of a clock.
Transfer printing Pattern transferred to ceramic on tissue paper.
Trefid, trifid Three lobed, as trefoil.
Trembleuse Saucer with raised central rim to hold cup in centre.
Tudric pewter With a shine like silver, used for 'Art Nouveau' wares from *c.*1902.
Tunbridge ware Marquetry boxes of 17th century and parquetry from *c.*1800.
Turned, turning Timber, metal, etc. shaped on a lathe in symmetrical circular motifs.
Twin train clock With a going train for movement and a striking train for chime.
Twist turned Asymmetrical turning of wood, etc. in barley-sugar twist.

Underglaze Pattern, colour, decoration applied to once-fired pottery and porcelain and then glazed.
Useful wares Denotes all but decorative and cabinet wares in pottery and porcelain.

Vandyke rim Scalloped like lace.
Veneer Thin sheets of wood shaped, cut and glued to carcase.
Verge escapement See Escapement.
Vesta case Match case.
Vinaigrette Small box with tightly fitting lid to hold scrap of aromatic sponge.
Vincennes Forerunner to famous Sèvres porcelain factory.
Vitreous Glass-like, with glass-like properties.
Vitruvian scroll Formalized S-scroll in wave pattern.
Volute Spiral scroll.

Waisted Straight or cylindrical shape curving inward like an hourglass.
Waiter A salver or tray.
Whatnot Tall extended form of dumb waiter with open shelves in tiers on central pillar or slender legs.
Wheel engraving Designs cut in glass with a revolving wheel and abrasive powder.
Whieldon, Thomas Staffordshire potter noted for development of marbled and mingled clays and glazes.
Williamite Period when William of Orange ruled alone from 1694–1702. Also in glass, period following Battle of the Boyne and establishment of Orange Order from *c.*1780.
Willow pattern Pseudo-Chinese design popularly used on early 19th-century pottery for tablewares.
Winding square The square, often shuttered, into which a clock key is inserted.
Windsor chair Hoop-backed solid wood chair, never veneered, with saddle seat, made in elm, oak, yew wood.
Wine cistern Large containers filled with ice or cold water in silver, marble, or lead or zinc-lined mahogany, often with a tap at the bottom to let out water.
Wine cooler Smaller versions of cisterns, often made in pairs for sideboards, in silver, mahogany, etc.
Wine taster Small, shallow, two-handled or two-eared bowl, usually Scottish or French, from 17th century.

Zaffre Saxony cobalt, blue pigment used for ceramic decoration from *c.*1545.

Bibliography

Furniture

Beard, Geoffrey. *National Trust Book of English Furniture*. Viking in association with the National Trust.

Duncan, Alastair. *Art Nouveau Furniture*. Thames & Hudson.

Feild, Rachael. *Buying Antique Furniture*. Macdonald & Co. (Publishers) Ltd.

Fleming, John. *The Penguin Dictionary of Decorative Arts*.

Gloag, John. *A Short Dictionary of Furniture*. George Allen & Unwin.

Lucie Smith, Edward. *Furniture: a Concise History*. Thames & Hudson.

Savage, George. *Dictionary of 19th century Antiques*. Barrie & Jenkins.

Wills, Geoffrey. *English Furniture*. Guinness Superlatives Ltd.

Clocks

Barker, David. *The Arthur Negus Guide to English Clocks*. Hamlyn.

Bird, Anthony. *English House Clocks 1600–1850*. David & Charles.

Brewer, Clifford. *The Country Life Collector's Pocket Book of Clocks*.

Loomes, Brian. *Complete British Clocks*. David & Charles.

Nicholls, A. *Clocks in Colour*. Blandford Press.

Smith, Alan. *The Guinness Book of Clocks*. Guinness Superlatives Ltd.

Symonds, R. W. *A History of English Clocks*. King Penguin.

Silver

Bannister, Judith. *The Country Life Collector's Pocket Book of Silver*.

Clayton, Michael. *The Collector's Dictionary of Silver and Gold*.

Culme, John. *Nineteenth-Century Silver*.

Luddington, John. *Starting to Collect Silver*. Antique Collectors' Club.

Rowe, Robert. *Adam Silver 1765 to 1795*.

Wardle, Patricia. *Victorian Silver and Silver-Plate*.

Wills, Geoffrey. *The Guinness Book of Silver*. Guinness Superlatives Ltd.

Pottery and Porcelain

Bembrose, G. *19th Century English Pottery & Porcelain*.

Fay-Hallé, A. and Barbara Mundt. *19th century European porcelain*. Trefoil Books Ltd.

Fisher, S. W. *English Pottery & Porcelain Marks*. W. Foulsham & Co.

Godden, Geoffrey. *Encyclopaedia of British Pottery & Porcelain*.

Hughes, G. Bernard. *The Country Life Collector's Pocket Book of China*.

Spero, Simon. *Worcester Porcelain*. Lund Humphries Publications.
Wills, Geoffrey. *English Pottery and Porcelain*. Guinness Superlatives Ltd.

Glass
Haynes, E. B. *Glass through the Ages*. Penguin Books.
Lattimore, Colin R. *English 19th Century Press-Moulded Glass*. Barrie and Jenkins.
Newman, Harold. *Illustrated Dictionary of Glass*.
Vane Percy, C. *The Glass of Lalique*. Trefoil Books Ltd.
Wills, Geoffrey. *English and Irish Glass*. Guinness Superlatives Ltd.
Wills, Geoffrey. *The Country Life Collector's Pocket Book of Glass*.

Index